Whither Indian Psychology?

Whither Indian Psychology?

Ajit K Dalal

RAWAT PUBLICATIONS
Jaipur • New Delhi • Bangalore • Guwahati • Kolkata

ISBN 978-81-316-1012-1

Published by
Prem Rawat for **Rawat Publications**
Satyam Apts., Sector 3, Jawahar Nagar, Jaipur 302 004 (India)
Phone: 0141 265 1748 / 7006 Fax: 0141 265 1748
E-mail: info@rawatbooks.com
Website: www.rawatbooks.com

New Delhi Office
4858/24, Ansari Road, Daryaganj, New Delhi 110 002
Phone: 011-23263290

Also at *Bangalore, Guwahati* and *Kolkata*

Typeset by Rawat Computers, Jaipur
Printed at Nice Printing Press, New Delhi

Contents

Preface

Three decades back when I went to University of California, Los Angeles (UCLA) for an year under Fulbright programme, many in the psychology department there wanted to know what kind of psychology I was doing back home. My mind was tuned to repeat that my field of research was attribution theory. There were many legendry figures at UCLA, including pioneers of the attribution theory. I thought my response would lead to exciting discussion on attribution work. But to my amazement that was a dampener. Some mustered courage to ask what kind of research was going on in my department which they have heard was a major centre of research in the country. My evasive answer often led to long silence or change of topic. I realized that psychology rooted in our own heritage and culture, was what people wanted to talk about. I knew little about it; Indian psychology was Western to the core. I started going to UCLA library and sat there for long hours to familiarize myself with the Indian scenario. Thereafter I talked at two universities on psychology in India.

On my return back to parent department from Fulbright, my interest in this area grew. It was a coincidence that about the same time I was offered a UNESCO project to write about the history of psychology in India. By that time, I was not aware that *psychology in India* and *Indian psychology* are two separate genres. Psychology in India deals with vast growth of Western psychology in India in the twentieth century and its development after Independence. Western psychology is held as universal science and is taught in universities of the most countries of the world. Indian psychology is referred to age-old knowledge system of mind, consciousness, and human behaviour. In modern times, ancient Indian knowledge system aimed to embark as a universal science of world peace, well-being, and human potential. With its own epistemology, methodology, and theoretical progress, Indian psychology aimed to consolidate Eastern knowledge base to develop as a composite science of humanity.

In the last three or four decades, Indian psychology grew rapidly, many important books came out, and conferences and meetings were held. It looked as if Indian psychology was coming of age. There was enthusiasm all around. But in last many years, the movement which was building up had started losing its vigour. The present academic scenario is chaotic in India. A debate is raging about the kind of psychology we need in India. We need to develop psychological knowledge which is relevant for twenty-first century India and which can deal with the problems of social unrest, war, depression, and suffering, and can thrive off human strength and positive transformation. Such an eclectic psychology should build on both Indian psychology and psychology in India to render discipline viable and relevant in the present times. We need to break new grounds to develop experimental and neurological psychology, whereas the ancient science of mind and consciousness can thrive on logical, intuitive, and yogic methodology. Only future will show how these ancient and modern psychologies could work in unison. There are many national and international precursors influencing progress of the discipline. In the present chaotic condition, we are still groping whither Indian psychology?

The book has six chapters. The first three chapters deal with history, content, and methodology of Indian psychology. The possibility of Indian psychology becoming a viable science with its own methodology, has been discussed in Chapter 4. Growth and expansion of psychology in India as a Western science has also been discussed in the same chapter. Chapter 5 deals with how history, culture, and society play a pivotal role in construction of knowledge and its perception by people. People in a society are both creator and construct of psychological world. The last chapter is a narration of my own journey through psychology as a discipline moving from Western brand of psychology to the psychology of Indian origin. For my generation, it took a lifetime to understand where we stand in this journey.

This book is written for researchers and teachers who intend to critically appraise the history of psychology as a discipline in this country. This book discusses where the psychology in India is heading and what future we envisage. It scans the socio-economic academic environment in which psychology is struggling to root itself. As a human science, its progress is contingent on local and international developments. This debate is raging all over the country and this book is expected to bring this deliberation to some fruition. This book should create a larger forum to deliberate on the place of social sciences in nation-building. In sense, the book should be useful to social scientists of different nomenclature.

Udaipur
August 2018

Ajit K Dalal

1

Indian Psychology

An Emerging Discipline

As one of the most ancient civilizations of the world, Indian subcontinent witnessed the evolution of an advanced system of knowledge some four to five millennia ago. This knowledge system thrived until the end of first century BC and travelled to the West through Middle East and to Tibet, China, and other Asian countries and Far East. Scholars from faraway places came to Indian educational centres to learn science, philosophy, and yoga. This knowledge system thrived till the end of first century BC when waves after waves of barbarians and fanatics devastated its flourishing knowledge culture. With subsequent decay of Indian civilization, its knowledge tradition weathered and remained stagnant for the next millennium. It was toward the last quarter of twenty-first century that the richness of Indian knowledge heritage caught the world's attention.

Sanskrit was the language in which scientific and philosophical knowledge was expounded. This body of knowledge is preserved in the scriptures compiled from time to time. These conceptual and theoretical formulations in old scriptures are not in the format and language in which contemporary scientific ethos are. They are imbedded in cultural ethos where no distinction is made in psychology, philosophy, and metaphysics. The theories have to be chiselled out from the existing scriptures and made comprehensible to the scientific community. That is the reason that they are largely ignored and kept out of the realm of mainstream science. A large body of this knowledge pertain to psychology of life and living, more precisely, about human mind and higher consciousness.

The theories of human mind formulated in the *Vedas* were further advanced and elaborated in *Upanishads* and later scriptures. Rooted in the Indian thought systems and practices, Indian psychology prospered as a holistic human science. In scriptures, these theories of mind and consciousness are presented in concise and precise verses, needing further explanation and elaboration. There are innumerable commentaries on the main texts brought out at different time points. The plurality of Indian intellectual tradition accommodates diverse perspectives varying from theism, i.e. different strands of spirituality, to atheism like Buddhism, Jain and Charvak schools. The remarkable thing is that all these schools of thought existed in harmony, without any history of conflict. The open intellectual environment furnished opportunities for creatively building alternative psychology which is Indian in origin but universal in its implications. This was the period when Indian civilization was at its peak, materially as well as spiritually. In its long march, Indian psychology made many breakthroughs in developing yogic techniques of self-control and of attaining higher level of human existence. These different schools of thoughts have their own premises, postulates, methodologies, and theoretical formulations. Of course, in the modern times, these theories need to be reformulated in present-day language of science and revalidated with newer methodologies developed.

Despite accommodation of atheistic schools all along its long history, Indian psychology continued as a science of consciousness. This consciousness is the substance which is the basis of our existence in this world. It is the substance which distinguishes living from non-living. Indian psychology does not subscribe to the Darwinian principle that man is developed form of ape; nor that man is a highly advanced machine. It premises the divine nature of human being, having a consciousness which is the same substance in all human beings, same in all living beings. Indian psychology has been built on universal values of peace and harmony with all living beings and nature. Indian psychology takes a position that human beings have free-will and are capable of attaining their higher existence. The highest goal of this psychology is to help people liberate themselves from the bondages of suffering and attain the state of bliss.

Clearly the methods of Western psychology, that are borrowed from physical sciences, are not very useful for testing propositions of the science of human consciousness. For scientific testing of the functioning of our inner selves, we need different kind of methodologies of yoga and meditation. Development of new methodologies is essential for the advancement of Indian psychology. It may be added here that for studying observable human behaviour Western methodology still has its relevance. The argument is not to reject it, but to employ it to material (empirical) level of human existence. That which is subtle can only be examined by honing the inner instrument. These techniques were mastered by Indian sages through rigorous training. Modern-day scientists doubt the authenticity of these techniques and even the presence of those phenomena. That is the reason parapsychology was not accepted as a scientific branch of psychology. Scientists don't understand how to examine intuition, premonition, and insight using the scientific methods which we know. These phenomena are better explained within the realm of spirituality.

A question often asked by students and teachers of psychology is, why is it important to study Indian psychology as a scientific discipline? Are we studying it as a philosophy and history of our glorious past, or as part of revivalist movement? We, in this book, see Indian psychology in a different light. It is a science which has much to contribute to the inner growth of a universal man, irrespective of religion, region, and nationality. How can one live a happy and meaningful life in a world where physical sciences have made strides in fields of communication, mobility, and physical comforts? Rapid development of science and technology in the present times has made life comfortable and opened up new opportunities to accomplish in this world. The modern science has not contributed to enriching the inner life. Inner growth is equally important to lead a meaningful life. Keeping in mind that Indian psychology is a practical science, it has much to offer to balance inner and outer domains and improve the quality of our being.

Indian psychology's focus on alleviation of human suffering by inner growth has much relevance in the world we are living. WHO reports clearly project that in the next one and half decade, about 50 per cent of the world population will be afflicted by depression, and suicide will be the number one killer disease in the world, superseding cancer and heart attack by 2030. How this horrific scenario can be handled by Western models of human development, no one knows. We need new models of human development and it is here that Indian psychology offers a hope.

Field of Indian Psychology

In the older times, Indian psychology was not conceived as a separate branch of psychological knowledge, it rather was spread in various spiritual, philosophical, medical, yogic, and astrological texts. Sages had composed texts on broader life domain, not exclusively devoted to mind and consciousness. There was resistance also to disconnect psychological concepts from the context in which they were embedded. It was only in the nineteenth century that some European Indologists tried to tease out psychological concepts from the classical texts. It is no surprise that the first *Handbook of Indian Psychology* was brought out in 2008 by Rao, Paranjpe, and Dalal. As Kiran Kumar has stated in his chapter in the Handbook, '... we do not find readily available models, theories, and systems of Indian psychology. So in creating a body of knowledge called Indian psychology, out of diverse sources, we face many problems like lack of clarity, lack of details, lack of compatibility, lack of continuity and such others, of ideas and views' (p. 19). Given such situation, contemporary efforts at carving out Indian psychology appear both challenging as well as perplexing.

Indian psychology is not one monolithic subject area; there are different schools subscribing to varying concepts and theories. Taken together they create a pattern in which one can see how different segments get integrated. There are varied schools of thoughts which originated and prospered in different times, and have survived in the long history. Even in the present times, Indian psychology is understood differently by different psychologists. The debate is still raging about what should constitute its subject field. To engage in this debate here will only confuse a naïve reader.

However, for the sake of clarity, in this book we will discuss two kinds of Indian psychologies, referred to as two broad traditions—classical (*shastriya*) tradition and folk (*loka*) tradition. The classical tradition is mostly subscribed by the elite or upper crust of the society. Theories and practices of human life developed by the elite and sages are documented in the classical texts (*shastras*). In India, within the classical tradition, there are wide range of schools and practices evolved in different zones and time periods. Folk traditions are subscribed primarily by the lower stratum of the society, peasants, and tribes whose social practices and rituals are mostly part of their oral culture. Both classical and folk traditions have been interacting in thousands of years' long history and are mutually enriching each other. In this long history, both traditions have come to share great epics and many of the social and religious practices, though there are many local variations. It may also be mentioned here that this wide diversity within classical and folk traditions are all part of a living, eclectic Indian culture. The cultural continuity across classical and folk traditions has led to the evolution of common consciousness among people at all levels. These two cultural traditions have grown, diversified, and survived through many challenges and upheavals, as they usher into the present age. Taken together, the knowledge base of these two traditions constitute what we are referring to as Indian psychology.

These knowledge traditions have evolved over centuries on materialistic, realistic, and spiritual philosophies propounded by sages and thinkers. Taking a holistic view of human life, Indian psychology makes no clear distinction among psychology, philosophy, sociology, and spirituality in formulation of theories of human consciousness and behaviour. Many view Indian psychology as 'science of human possibilities and progression'. It has nurtured a worldview informed by continuity, interdependence, and connectivity across all life forms—from unicellular amoeba to multicellular human beings. Indian psychology emphasizes an inclusive notion of socio-spiritual field rather than taking individuals as the centre of existence. By situating humans in the wider space–time continua, Indian psychology offers a whole range of theories and concepts pregnant with exciting hypotheses about human nature, modalities of worldly engagements, and developmental stages. Indian psychology has evolved through rigorous observation, experimentation, and reflection through training under *gurus*, continuous contemplation, and sharing of personal accounts of inner experiences.

It needs to be made explicit that the purpose of identifying, developing, and testing Indian concepts and theories is to not to assert their superiority but to examine their relevance for the modern world. It is a theoretical and methodological movement to examine our heritage and to develop testable propositions. The endeavour is to contemporize Indian psychological theories and test their relevance for enhancing human potential, well-being, and by that, making this world a better place to live.

Indian psychology has originated and prospered in the geographical region of Indian subcontinent. Its premises are compatible with the cultural and social life of the region, though these have never been restricted to people of Indian subcontinent only. Indian psychology aspires to focus on the upliftment of humanity in general, irrespective of creed, region, and culture, not just of people of Indian origin. Indian psychology thrived on the protest movements, such as Buddhism and Jainism, and also on other philosophies of the region, such as Taoism, Zoroastrianism, and Sufism. Its influence in the ancient times was far beyond the borders of greater India; Indian psychology was in communion with other contemporary philosophies of the East, such as Tao and Zen Buddhism, and this mutual influence is very much visible even today. These philosophies provided the intellectual and spiritual firmament to generate new ideas and explanations, as evident in post-*Upanishad* texts (such as Shankar's non-dualism). Theories and practices of Indian psychology address wider existential issues—purpose and significance of human life. Thus, though the term 'Indian psychology' implies a psychology of Indian origin, or a psychology that has grown in the Indian subcontinent, it purports to be a universal science of humanity.

In this backdrop, it is just a coincidence that the term Indian psychology is used in last century by the pioneers in this field, like Jadunath Sinha who brought out three volumes entitled *Indian Psychology* (1933–58); Rhys Davids' book, *The Birth of Indian Psychology and its Development in Buddhism* (1936); Raghunath

Safaya's *Indian Psychology* (1975); and B. Kuppuswami's book *Elements of Ancient Indian Psychology* (1985). The later addition to this sequel being the *Handbook of Indian Psychology* by Rao, Paranjpe, and Dalal (2008); *Foundations of Indian Psychology* by Cornelissen, Misra, and Varma (2011); *Psychology and Psychoanalysis* by Misra (2014); and *Psychology in Indian Tradition* by Rao and Paranjpe (2015). In essence, Indian psychology is not a study of Indian people, as its nomenclature may give an impression; it is a science of human nature and life in its all diversities.

Is Indian Psychology a Science?

It is important to address this question at the initial stage of this book to set this issue at rest. Western psychology was being established in the Indian universities as the mainstream psychology during the British rule. N.N. Sengupta who established the first psychology department at the Calcutta University fought hard and succeeded in locating it as the science faculty, as the Department of Experimental Psychology. The same Western psychology continued as the mainstream psychology in all departments of psychology throughout the country even after 60–70 years of Independence. The main argument in favour of Western psychology is that its credentials as a science are well established. Research and teaching in the domain of Indian psychology remained confined within the philosophy departments of the academic institutions, as it was not considered a science. It is only in the recent decades that Indian psychology is gradually recognized as an independent field of scientific study.

However, this debate, whether Indian psychology is a science, or a subject matter of cultural, spiritual, and philosophical discourse, has not subsided till date. A large number of Indian psychologists still consider Indian psychology as mystical, enigmatic, and occult, and thus beyond the realm of scientific investigation. Indian psychology being embedded in the spiritual tradition of India also goes against considering it as science. Many consider it as being part of the religious movement polluting the secular culture of academic institutions. This scenario is only gradually changing and Indian psychology is getting acceptance as a science, like other branches of social sciences.

In the broadest sense, science is a systematic pursuit of knowing the world through the methods of observation and experimentation. Psychological research deals with objective observation of both the worlds—the world which is outside and the world which is inside a person. This outside world belongs to the physical environment which extends from subatomic to supergalactic entities which influences all of us in some known and unknown ways. This physical world is primarily studied in natural sciences. The other domain of outside world is the social world, comprising family, social groups, communities, political and spiritual organizations, created by us but which shape our lives. The methods of physical sciences are employed to study both physical and social world we live in. The third domain of research is the inside world of a person, comprising her or his attitudes, values, socialization, relationships, feelings, and strivings. Since human beings are capable of sharing their experiences, empirical methods of physical sciences are modified in due course in Western psychology and new methods were evolved within the framework of objectivity, measurement, and verifiability. From the Indian psychological perspective there is a fourth domain of study, that is, consciousness, which defines our existence and is universal. Knowledge about this consciousness has been a major preoccupation of Indian sages and scholars.

While viewing Indian approach to science, few points need to be understood. One, Indian science and spirituality are not seen as antithetical to each other. These are taken as complementary and overlapping approaches to know the truth. There is no history of conflict between science and spirituality in India as witnessed in the West in the Age of Enlightenment. Second, the world is believed to be governed by some natural laws of the universe which explain the attributes of the matter and energy, as well as that of mind and consciousness. In fact, what we consider as material world is held as the manifestation of supreme consciousness. Third, a distinction is made between two types of sciences—science that seeks knowledge of the self and science, that seeks knowledge of the world. These two types of knowledge are distinguished as *pāra vidyā* and *apāra vidyā* in the *Manduk Upanishad*. *Parā vidyā* is knowledge of the supreme consciousness (self) which constitutes our true existence; on the other hand, *apāra vidya* is the knowledge of the world we live in. Though knowledge of the self is considered to be of prime importance, both types of knowledge are considered essential to function in this mundane world. Fourth, methods of knowing the self primarily relied on yoga and meditation through which the mind can be silenced to know the truth. A quiet mind is the best instrument to perceive one's true self. The outside world can be known through human senses and scientific instruments developed. A quiet mind can also be an effective instrument to know the external world. The *Yoga Sutras* of Maharishi Patanjali enumerates the stages and practices to silence the mind and attain the state of *samadhi*. These aspects will be discussed in detail later. Fifth, Indian tradition always focussed on knowing the knower. It was considered important to know the person who is seeking knowledge and how best that person can train own-self for that knowledge. It also envisages a situation in which knowledge and knower becomes one.

Indian psychology is an applied and practical science which leads to testable hypotheses and methodologies aiming at inner transformation of the human being. Many of its propositions cannot be tested by the accepted methods of science but require a broad spectrum of methodologies from the spiritual domain. The field grew in tradition of critical examination where scholars and sages continuously proposed, analysed, interpreted, refined, and transmitted knowledge to the worthy disciples. It is remarkable that these institutions survived all along the history without much State support. Apparently Indian psychology as a field of knowledge is rooted in philosophy (*Darshana*), life science (*Āyurveda*), social and moral studies (*Dharma Shāstra, Neeti, Artha Shāstra, Kāma Shāstra*), spirituality (*Ādhyātma Vidyā*), Jain, Buddhist, Sufic, and other socio-spiritual movements and folk practices.

As mentioned earlier human science and technology was flourishing in India till the end of the first century. There were many centres of education all across the country. The Nalanda University was a major centre of education and research in the Eastern India. With the decimation of these centres of knowledge in the eleventh century, a Dark Age in Indian intellectual history began which perpetuated till the beginning of twentieth century. During this period, mass-scale destruction and decline of science occurred in India which led to the sorry state today. In this period, there was hardly any new school or new theory developed in the field of Indian psychology. The need of the hour is, rather than eulogizing the past, to pick up threads from the past and continue developing Indian psychology as a relevant science in the present times. In this sense, Indian psychology in its present reincarnation as a science of human life is still at an early stage of its growth.

Domains of Indian Psychology

Indian psychology does not have consensually accepted boundaries, demarcated by an agreed-upon content field. Indian psychology is viewed differently by its proponents. Some view it as a repository of Indian psychological knowledge inherent in the classical texts. Subscribers of this view emphasize relevance of this body of knowledge as a school of psychology with its own theories and methodologies. The effort is to project it as a universal science, as an alternative to the Western psychology. Others view it as indigenous psychology, on par with other indigenous psychologies of Asian, African, and Latin American regions, including the psychology of subaltern societies. These indigenous psychologies are seen as independent, yet auxiliary to the mainstream (Western) psychology. This group strives to integrate Indian psychology within the mainstream psychology. There is still another group of psychologists who consider Indian psychology not as a content field but as a movement to develop an alternative psychology which is universal in its framework while dealing with the local issues. The idea is to transform research and teaching of psychology in India and make it more compatible with Indian social reality and cultural ethos. These three viewpoints posit Indian psychology in rather different mould.

In the Indian knowledge system, the person is the central focus, the world (*sansar*) in which she or he lives is of secondary importance. The person is believed to be constituted of consciousness, mind, and body. Consciousness is awareness of one's existence in this world and is non-physical. Mind is a hypothetical construct considered to be responsible for cognitive functions of thinking, perceiving, and inferring. On one side it is linked with consciousness and on the other side with body. Both mind and body are considered to be physical. Mind being made of subtle matter, whereas body is of gross. Mind communicates with consciousness but does not influence it; whereas mind and body closely interact, one influencing the other. The purpose of the life is to liberate mind of its conditioning and sensory bondage so that it becomes an instrument of consciousness.

Rao and Paranjpe (2015) held Indian psychology as the science of consciousness. The consciousness in Indian psychology is considered to be the highest state of human existence. It is the state of being of an individual which connotes one's true existence, beyond the physical existence. In this sense the terms being, Brahman, self, and consciousness are often used interchangeably, implying highest level of spiritual existence. However, different schools of thought in India vary in their conception of consciousness. But these schools converge on four attributes of consciousness. One, it is pure state of being which is content-less, formless, and self-illumined, often called consciousness-as-such. Two, it is transcendental in nature, meaning it is subjectivity beyond the dichotomy of subject–object, and consequently beyond the distinction of the knower and the object of knowledge. Three, this is not hypothetical state but one is often aware of its presence. This is trans-cognitive state, meaning thereby, it is not part of our sensory experience. This consciousness acquires knowledge of the reality directly and can communicate it when the mind it quiet. Four, it illuminates the mind by its presence, and consequently, is aware of the activities of the mind. It neither directs, nor is affected by the mind and life experiences. The consciousness remains an uninvolved observer and witness to the play of life.

The other kind of consciousness is called transactional, transitional, or phenomenological. It is the embodied consciousness. It is the consciousness which is characterized by conscious–unconscious dichotomy, and also by distinction between subject–object and among knower–knowing–knowledge, as in the Western psychology. It is the state of cognition of inside (thoughts, feelings, and images) and outside world (people, object, and situations). This knowledge is acquired through sensory–motor modalities of human being. Commonly, it is referred to as waking consciousness, which is awareness of the world we live in. Western psychology has primarily confined itself to this waking consciousness borne out of the sensory experience. Quite often when Western and Indian theories of consciousness are compared without acknowledging this distinction, such research and teaching add to confusion rather than to the knowledge.

It may be mentioned here that both transcendental and transactional consciousness are combined in the four stages of consciousness, as discussed in the *Manduk Upanishad*. These four stages of consciousness are *jagrat* (wakeful), *swapna* (dream), *sushupti* (deep sleep), and *turia* (often called the fourth stage of consciousness). The first three stages are transactional while the fourth one is transcendental. *Jagrat* state is that state of consciousness in which one is aware of the objects of the mundane world one live in. In dream state, the attention is diverted inward and one perceives the images projected by the mind. In the *sushupti* state, the consciousness is completely withdrawn inside and one is not aware of inner and outer world. The fourth state of consciousness is free from object relationship and perception of duality as the mind attains quietude. A person becomes one with the universal consciousness; it is the consciousness-as-such without any content.

Indian psychology builds on both the modes of knowing, with greater emphasis on transcendental knowing. These two modes of knowing are also characterized as *parā vidyā* (knowledge of the self) and *aparā vidyā* (empirical knowledge). *Aparā vidyā* constitutes of the knowledge of the social–physical world we live in and includes science and technology. This knowledge is also relevant to the problems and challenges of the world we live in. The methods of knowing in the empirical world (*pramāṇa*) are diverse and they treat mind (*mānas* or *antaḥkaranā*) as one sensory channel, which allows the understanding of pleasure and pain. *Para vidya* is the knowledge of one's higher existence, beyond the empirical world. It is the knowledge of one's higher consciousness; knowledge of that which is permanent and imperishable. Here not only the very 'object' of knowledge is very different, but even the approach and methodologies are different.

These two modes of knowing, taken together, cover the whole range of human existence and experiences. They cover from mundane life experiences to awareness of our higher existence. As one ascends to higher stages of mental evolution, from mundane to spiritual, one comes in contact with higher consciousness which unites one with all humanity and universal truth. The same conception holds at both elite and folk strata of the society. Even common men are aware and are capable of attaining higher state of consciousness. Indian psychology in this sense is a science of human life, dealing with all domains of everyday living in the physical world, as well with existence at higher, non-physical level, and how these two modes of living can be assimilated in one's life.

Within this broad classificatory framework of transcendental and transactional consciousness, the term is understood by different schools of thought in India. The Sankhya school sees it in terms of *purush–prakriti* dichotomy. *Purush* stands for consciousness. Its main text, the *Sankhya Karika*, postulates multiple *purush*, one for each person. These *purushas* are pure consciousness, indifferent, inactive, and silent witness of what a person is doing, thinking, or feeling. On the other hand, this pure consciousness is called *Brahman* in *Advait Vedant* of Shankar which is self-illuminating, undifferentiated, unintentional, and not limited by space and time. It is pervasive in all human beings. All Indian schools make a distinction between consciousness and mind, where mind is part of the *prakriti* which is though illuminated by consciousness but limited, qualified, and embodied by individual existence. Mind is supposed to contain memories of all past actions, tendencies, intentions, and volitions. This mind, sometimes called 'manas', is built on sensory experiences, and is behind all human actions. Sri Aurobindo developed a comprehensive stage theory of mind in the first quarter of last century, evolving from manas to supramental state of existence.

It can be argued that all scientific theories are built on some basic assumptions about nature and reality. Western sciences (psychology in particular) are also built on a long tradition of socio-religious beliefs and practices of Europe. These assumptions are never questioned but without understanding these assumptions psychological theories would not make sense. For example, hedonism (that man seeks pleasure and avoids pain) is at the core of many social learning theories. Assumptions are the statements of faith that determine the methodology to be employed and conclusions to be drawn. The behaviouristic psychology considered man as a machine, which suited its mechanistic models of learning and behaviour. The metaphor of the 'man as computer' changed the concerns and methodology of research, taking the human being as information processor. Similarly, the metaphor, 'man as pure consciousness' holds human being as capable of rising above their physical limitations and attaining their transcendental state. The 'man as pure consciousness' metaphor calls for a different ontological and epistemological position in formulation of research questions, which in many cases need different methodology. Within this framework, the *Bhagavad Gita* propositions based on this metaphor in Indian psychology should be testable and experientially verifiable.

Differentiating Indian Psychology from Related Fields

As mentioned earlier a distinction is generally made being between *Indian psychology* (psychology of Indian origin) and *psychology in India* (academic/Western psychology in India). Part of the problem stems from the fact that in other social sciences such a distinction is of little consequence. For example, Indian sociology, or Indian philosophy are same as sociology or philosophy in India. These terms were coined by the British scholars who were engaged in studying Indian society and philosophy in the later part of eighteenth century. Moreover, Indian sociology and Indian philosophy as academic disciplines have a long history of more than 150 years and there is no misconception about their subject matter. This is not so in the case of Indian psychology. *Psychology in India* has a history that spans the beginning of the last century, but in comparison, Indian psychology is still struggling to establish itself in the academic portals.

Indian psychology has emerged as a domain of serious research in academia only in the preceding two decades. Its contours and content are still in the process of evolving and there is lack of clarity about its subject domain. In fact, courses on Indian psychology were introduced in many Indian universities (e.g. BHU, Mysore, Jodhpur, and Andhra Universities) in the mid-60s. These courses were primarily imported from philosophy and their subject matter and pedagogy were incompatible with the general ethos of psychology departments, which was more tuned to laboratory research. Courses on Indian psychology, therefore, could not survive for long and within a decade they were withdrawn from most places. Incidentally, the view still persists that Indian psychology is nothing but Indian philosophy.

This is yet another reason why Indian psychology is not part of the academic curriculum at most of the Indian universities.

In this backdrop it is quite natural to encounter many misconceptions about what Indian psychology stands *for*, and what it does *not*. To offer Indian psychology as psychological knowledge rooted in Indian cultural heritage and scriptures dating back to more than three millennia and claiming its relevance to the contemporary world is unconvincing to many. As a growing science of Indian origin, Indian psychology is often held as a conglomeration of several, sometimes even contradictory, fields of investigation. The edifice of Indian psychology constitutes distinct ontology, epistemology, and methodology. Many proponents of Indian psychology consider only classical texts of consciousness and yoga as valid subject matter. They do include elaboration of classical texts by the modern thinkers as well. Folk (*loka*) psychology is conspicuously avoided in such deliberations. It is debatable whether folk traditions should, or should not constitute part of the Indian psychology. Though some Indian psychologists are in favour of it, but they are in minority. The contours of Indian psychology are still forming and one cannot take a firm stand on this issue. To arrive at some clarity about the subject matter of Indian psychology, there is a need to compare it from similar fields of study. In the following section some such fields of study which overlap with Indian psychology will be scrutinized.

Psychology of Indian People

Due to common historical, social, and cultural background it is natural that Indian people share many dispositional and behavioural characteristics. On the very grounds, Indian people would differ from Americans, Chinese, or any other ethnic group. Studies of these cultural differences have been a very productive area of research in cross-cultural psychology. Being primarily a methodological field, cross-cultural psychology has taken the *etic* approach to establish equivalence of psychological phenomena for cross-cultural comparisons (Berry, 1989). On the other side is the *emic* approach, employed when culture-specific phenomenon are investigated.

Both cross-cultural psychology and cultural psychology have examined how Indian people differ from other cultural groups.

Using personality tests, efforts are made to identify core characteristics of Indian people. These findings are often empirical generalizations and tend to make sweeping statements about the populations under investigation. Given India's vast ethnic diversity, these studies often fail to unravel enduring patterns and differences. Such research often ends up creating stereotypes about cultural groups. For example, India is often viewed as a collective culture. Such findings are at best tentative—interpretable only within a space–time matrix. On the other hand, Indian psychology endeavours to identify enduring human attributes. It is search for human ontology which is atemporal and transcultural, particularly with growth potential for transcendence.

Study of Ancient Indian Wisdom

Indian psychology is not merely a historical documentation of the ancient Indian wisdom. Indian civilization is one of the most ancient civilizations of the world and has a vast treasure house of knowledge and wisdom that has remained hidden and inaccessible to academic psychology. As academic psychology in India has begun to explore this symbolic and conceptual resource, it has opened up varied possibilities of exciting research propositions. It may be relevant to add in this context that this ancient knowledge has been extended, elaborated, and even questioned in the long history. Thinkers and sages of modern times have added and commented on what we know from *Vedas*, *Upanishads*, and different schools of thought. Sri Aurobindo, Ramakrishna, Krishnamurthi, and Gandhi are names of a few modern thinkers who have vastly contributed to this ancient wisdom and have been able to present it in a language which we understand. This knowledge base has potential to make this world a better place to live and constitute integral part of Indian psychology.

Indian psychology is not revivalist, if revivalism means reassertion of the ancient order in the present world. It cannot be an exercise to reaffirm the theories propounded in the ancient texts employing scientific methodology, nor does it aim to establish its superiority over other knowledge systems. The challenge before Indian psychology is to carve out the testable propositions emanating from this ancient wisdom and develop appropriate methodology to test them. The study of ancient human science is not merely an academic exercise but it aims to transform self and build a happy, healthy, and harmonious social order. Indian psychology is part of a movement toward contemporizing Indian theories and testing their relevance for enhancing human competencies and well-being.

Indigenous Psychology

D. Sinha (1994) reminded us about two types of indigenization. The first is an outcome of adaptation of the mainstream (Western) psychology to a different cultural setup. A large body of research in India can be included in this kind of indigenization in which cultural concepts and practices are examined as employing Western theories and approaches. A large number of Western tests of personality, intelligence, motives, values, health, and well-being are indigenized taking this approach. Such indigenization is likely to continue in a global world where there is a constant flow of models and concepts across cultures, particularly from the West. The other kind of indigenization is that which is based on a systematic analysis of culture-bound concepts and categories. Such indigenization focuses on the contemporary relevance of cultural heritage and native theories which come within the rubric of 'Indian psychology'. Misra and Mohanty's Volume (2002) *Perspectives on Indigenous Psychology* includes Indian research that belongs to both the categories. Srivastava and Misra (2003) have undertaken the study of intelligence which is an example of the second kind of indigenization. They use multiple sources, that is, traditional texts, popular idioms, and lay people's understanding and usage to develop a new model of intelligence. Indigenous psychology, in this sense, is synonymous to folk psychology, a discipline that has evolved in a particular societal context, which is used by lay people to organize and conduct of their lives. However, Indian psychology has panhuman interest even while dealing with local cultures.

A Note on the Western Psychology

Before we proceed further it is important to understand parallel developments in the West, to build a historical context in which Indian psychology is trying to find its foothold.

The origin of Western psychology is mostly traced to Greek philosophy. The word psychology itself is derived from the Greek words 'psyche' which means soul and 'logos' which means study. Psychology thus started as a study of soul, which later turned into the study of mind, and remained part of the moral and philosophical discourse for almost two millennia.

Plato and Aristotle were among the first philosophers in the West who turned to systematic study of the mind. Plato postulated that the body and the mind are two independent entities and that the mind could exist even after death. This stance was not acceptable to his disciple Aristotle, who though accepted the premise of the body–mind duality but did not believe that education can change the basic nature of human beings. The premises of Plato and Aristotle were at the centre of discourses and philosophical writings about human mind for almost two millennia. Rene Descartes, the French philosopher and mathematician, in seventeenth century accepted the body–mind duality, though he accepted that there is a continuous transaction between the body and the mind through penal gland.

In the eighteenth century AD, John Locke, a British political philosopher, proposed that thinking is not innate and knowledge is accumulated through the sensory experiences. He believed that human mind is a clean slate at the time of birth. These were the basic ideas on which modern Western psychology grew in the later period.

Credit for separating psychology from philosophy is given to William Wundt, who started Institute of Experimental Psychology at Lipzig, Germany in 1879. Using introspection method in experimental work, his endeavour was to identify the basic structure of psychological experiences. He is credited with the beginning of the school of structuralism in psychology which focussed on the structure of human consciousness. Study of consciousness provided continuity between Greek philosophies and new psychology with scientific methods. However, introspection method was criticized as too subjective and was discarded when psychology moved from Western Europe to North America. American psychology deemphasized experimental introspection in favour of comparative and empirical methods taken from physical sciences. These new schools, functionalism and behaviourism, changed the subject matter of psychology from consciousness to observable behaviour. William James's book *Principles of Psychology* (1890) is considered to be the first comprehensive textbook in psychology.

European psychology continued to be rooted in its socio-historical ethos where Freudian and neo-Freudian psychoanalytical schools grew in the first half of the last century. Freud drew extensively from Greek mythology to develop his theory of unconscious mind. Freud's work revolutionized the treatment of mental disorders. However, Freudian theory was considered speculative, scientifically unverifiable, and therefore, largely ignored by the later schools. That was the time when behaviourism was in ascendance and it primarily focussed on the study of overt and observable behaviour. Research during this period was primarily conducted on animals, whose behaviour can be easily controlled and manipulated in experimental setting. Work of Watson, Pavlov, Skinner, and Guthrie was significant in developing theories of learning and perception. Another school which was coming in existence by this time was that of cognitive psychology with the Piaget's *Stage Theory of Cognitive Development*, Chomsky work on language behaviour, and Neisser's book *Cognitive Psychology*. Piaget's work on children's learning and thinking inspired more research than that of any other theorists till date. Chomsky rejected Skinner's theory of verbal learning and argued that children's language behaviour is not a learned response but can produce infinite variety of sentences varying in meaning and structure once they develop their internal mental structure. Neisser characterized people as information-processing systems whose mental operations might be described in computational terms.

Growth of humanistic school with Maslow's *Need Hierarchy Theory* was another major development in the history of psychology. Humanistic school stressed phenomenological approach to study human experiences. Many humanistic psychologists reject scientific approach, arguing that human experiences cannot be measured as inanimate objects in physical sciences and preferred qualitative approach in their research. Frankel's logotherapy and Roger's *Client-Centred Therapy* are other salient contributions to this school. The later offshoots of this school were existential psychology and transpersonal psychology which brought non-sensory and transcendental experiences into the realm of psychology. Maslow's emphasis on happiness and mental health rather than on mental illness has inspired many, which led to a new school of positive psychology in the twenty-first century. Seligman and Mihali are given credit for this new school which emphasized on positive human functioning, and to develop effective interventions to build thriving in individuals, families, and communities. Positive psychology is a new turn in Western psychology in the present times. Despite this change in emphasis, positive psychology is very much entrenched in the empirical tradition of Western psychology, which has continued for 100 years.

In practice, most Western psychologists have an eclectic outlook on psychology. They often draw on ideas and theories from different schools rather than holding to any singular perspective. This is not the occasion to discuss these different schools and their implications for the development of Western psychology. However, it is important to note that American and Western European psychology has often been portrayed as a universal form of psychology which can be relevant in any part of the world. This psychology put the issues related to cultural orientation including that of marginalized societies on periphery. Secondly, there is a heavy reliance on scientific methods, primarily on experiments and psychological testing, specifically on quantification and empirical verification. This reliance on scientific methods was so much that quite often the methods dictated the objectives of inquiry in psychological research. Western psychology still dominates the world scenario and is considered mainstream psychology in most of the countries.

Table 1.1 presents a comparison of Western and Indian psychology.

Table 1.1

A Comparison of Western and Indian Psychology

Western Psychology	*Indian Psychology*
Material, physicalist	Spiritual
Reductionist (biological)	Transcendental (higher existence)
Dualism—mind–body	Dualism—*purush–prakriti*
Self, sensory mind	Self, higher consciousness
Overt behaviour, surface consciousness	Inner knowledge, awareness
Objective	Subjective
Measurement, quantitative	Immeasurable, qualitative,
Knowledge—informative, constructive	Knowledge—transformative
Distinguishes theory and practice	Inseparable, practical knowledge
Third-person methodology	First-person methodology

History of Indian Psychology

Like all other ancient sciences, Indian psychology has no fixed beginning. Many of the concepts and concerns which went into the formation of Indian psychology are pre-Aryans, embedded in the oral culture of that period. From the time immemorial, Indian sages and thinkers were struck by the immensity of the universe and inexhaustible mystery of human life. In the Vedic texts it was held that the universe has evolved out of that *One*. This first principle of 'that One' (*tad ekam*) is considered to be indescribable. It is without qualities or attributes, neither positive nor negative. Any attempt to describe it, is to delimit and bind that which is limitless and unbounded. This conception of universe is very similar to presently accepted scientific theory of the origin of universe. It may be mentioned in this context that the *Vedic* seers admitted in all humility that this proposition about the creation was only a surmise, for it is not possible to be sure of the events that occurred in the distant past.

However, this notion of unity in diversity and seeing no contradiction between the opposites (e.g. good–bad) is one of the core principles of Indian psychology. Within this broad principle, Indian thinkers exercised freedom to interpret and elaborate the text(s) in different ways. The *Upanishads* are not the thoughts of a single thinker; they evolved over a period of time through scholarly discourses and contemplations. In *Upanishads*, the interest is shifted from objective to the subjective, from outside world to the Self, in whose infinite depths the universe is reflected in its entirety. *Upanishads* discuss at length the path of the inner ascent, the inward journey toward ultimate reality. The diversity of ideas, concepts, and visions encapsulated in the verses of *Upanishads* has inspired generations of thinkers and has laid the foundations of Indian psychology.

It is conceded in the *Vedas* and other texts that the absolute and infinite cannot be known through the imperfect human mind. What is known about life and existence is therefore conjectural, logical, and intuitive in most of the cases. Scepticism and questioning is very much built-in in the mode of inquiry in the *Ṛig Veda* itself. Even the existence of Indra, the king of gods, is questioned. 'Of whom they ask, where is he? Of him, they also say, he is not.' (*Ṛig Veda* II 12). Such doubts are frequently raised throughout the classical texts, though the quest to know absolute and infinite remains paramount till date. Systematic dialogue (*samvād*) has been a potent method of advancing understanding about life and the universe. In the case of testing premises about self and transcendental knowledge, methods of self-verification were developed. This tradition of questioning and free thinking provided impetus to Indian psychology for centuries, and with many ups and downs and setbacks, it kept prospering till the recent times.

Upanishads were composed in a 1,000-year period, but definitely before eighth or seventh centuries BC, much before the arrival of Buddha and Mahavir. These scriptures are mostly in the form of dialogues between a *guru* and *shishyas* about truth, Brahman life and universe. In that ancient tradition, the students would live with their teacher and imbibe an outlook to life that would resonate with the sage's teaching. The idea being that knowledge is not to be separated from daily life, but must also become practical. There are 200-known *Upanishads*, of them only 14 are frequently referred to. They are *Aitareya*, *Brhadaranyaka*, *Chandogya*, *Isa*, *Katha*, *Kena*, *Kausitaki*, *Maitri*, *Mandukya*, *Mahanarayana*, *Mundaka*, *Prasna*, *Svetasvatara*, and *Taittiriya*. These are called the principal *Upanishads*. In the Indian spiritual tradition little distinction is made between psychology, philosophy and metaphysics, and these *Upanishads* cover the whole range of human concerns. The opening question (1.1.3) in the *Mundaka Upanishad* best illustrates the primary concern of all the *Upanishads*, where a student asks the sage, 'What is that by knowing which everything is known?' The *Mundaka Upanishad* dialogues on this fundamental philosophical question which triggers further questions such as 'What is knowledge' and 'What do we mean by knowing?' Another fundamental question asked was, 'how can the knower be known?'

The essential purpose of *Upanishads* is to stimulate reflection and queries. They often raise questions about the meaning of words and concepts, even of the commonly used terms. As meaning of such words is open to question, so is the interpretation of *Upanishads*. *Upanishads* are monistic, or more accurately, profess non-dualism. There is no reference to the God in Upanishadic writings, though some phrases are misinterpreted in some commentaries to imply presence of the God. Dualism is rooted in the separation of me and you, or me and God. Non-dualism of *Upanishads* implies that this universe is pervaded by the cosmic ruling force, and in fact, every particle of it, is that, nothing belongs to me. Thus, we are to enjoy this world by giving up the sense of ownership and by being an observer. It is the mind which creates the dichotomy of the observer and the observed, of the knower and the known. It is through the sensory experience that appearance of an objective world takes shape, as different from me as an observer.

At about the same time when different *Upanishads* were composed, six different psycho-philosophical schools also came into existence. These schools of thoughts are *Nyaya*, *Vaisheshika*, *Yoga*, *Samkhya*, *Purva Mimamsa*, and *Vedanta*. Each school has a set of *sutras* or aphorisms that forms its nucleus and gives the essential teaching of the school. The first four of these schools accept the authority of the *Vedas,* but do not derive their philosophical principles from the statements of the *Vedas.* They are based on the teachings of individual *rishis* or sages. The remaining two schools, *Purva Mimamsa* and *Vedanta*, have taken a good deal from the four *Vedas*.

These six *darshanas* (or schools) are termed *astika* philosophies (from *asti*, or 'it is so'), because they all acknowledge the *Vedas* as authoritative, as opposed to the *nastika* philosophies of the Carvakas, Buddhists, and Jains (*nasti*, 'it is not so'), believed in action for obtaining things of this world and the next; and the first two parts of the *Veda* contain their ideas, on which the *Mimamsa* philosophy is based. As these ideas are the earliest, the *Mimamsa* philosophy is given first in this book. This was originally the true orthodox tradition.

The *Sankhya* is the oldest among these schools. *Sankhya* literary means numbers, the number of elements of which the life is composed of, and this is what the *Sankhya* school has discussed at length. The two basic elements are *purush* and *prakriti* and their union is the basis of this world. The first modification of *prakriti* is called *mahat* or the cosmic intelligence. This further evolves into *ahankara* or ego; *ahankara* gives rise to mind. This conception that the mind is mechanical and evolves from ego, has significant practical implications. The *Yoga* school, which is the most popular among all, has much in common with the *Sankhya* school. According to *Yoga*, the *manas*, the sensory mind selectively records the available information which is cognized and interpreted by the ego, and then assimilated by the *buddhi* to have a phenomenal (perceived) awareness of the world we live in. Obviously such perception of the world and events by the mind is subjective and biased. When the mind is deconditioned through yoga and is illuminated by the consciousness, it sees the reality as such. Patanjali's *Yoga Sutra* enumerates step-by-step procedure to transcend phenomenal reality to see the reality as such.

The *Nyaya* school is primarily concerned with the conditions of correct knowledge and the means of receiving this knowledge. The *Nyaya* is predominantly based on reasoning, logic and methods of knowing, and therefore is also known as *Nyaya vidya* or *Tarka Sastra*. *Nyaya* sets up the rules of philosophical debate and asserts that obtaining valid knowledge of the external world and its relationship with the mind and self is the only way to attain liberation. The *Vaisesika* school is allied to the *Nyaya* school, as both systems accept the liberation of the individual self as the ultimate goal; both view ignorance as the root cause of all pain and suffering; and both believe that liberation is attained only through right knowledge. The *Vaisesika* accepts perception and inferences as the method of deeper analysis of the predicament of material existence. According to the *Vaisesika*, as external sense faculties are necessary for the perception of external objects of the world, an internal sense faculty of mind is required for the perception of internal objects, such as self, thinking, feeling, pleasure, and pain.

The word '*Mimamsa*' means to analyse and understand thoroughly. The *Mimamsa* and *Vedanta* schools are closely related to each other and are in some ways complimentary. The *Mimamsa* school examines the teachings of the *Veda* in terms of rituals, whereas *Vedanta* examines the same teachings in terms of transcendental knowledge. The performance of Vedic rituals is intended to remind one's of the significance of life duties and dharma. *Vedanta* means culmination of Vedic knowledge. Shankar's *Advaita Vedanta* is in some ways extension of the Vedic philosophy.

Both Buddhism and Jainism rejected the *Vedas* as scriptural authorities, and can be seen as protest movements against ritualistic and rigid social hierarchy and maintained their hegemony of the Brahmin class. The proponents of these two schools were contemporary in sixth century BC. The scriptures of both the schools were written in Prakrit and Pali languages. These two schools shared their metaphysics and yet differed in important ways. Buddhism took a more pragmatic approach and had greater mass following than Jainism. Jainism remained more rigid in following the principle of *ahimsa* (non-violence) and shunned violence of any kind.

The *Carvaka* school, also known as *lokayata* philosophy, is a heterodox school named after its founder and often classified with its fellow dissenter philosophies of Buddhism and Jainism. However, unlike Jainism and Buddhism, *Carvaka* has not turned into its own religious sect and remains a philosophical ideal. Being an atheist school, *Carvaka* rejects authority of the *Vedas* as revealed texts (*sruti*) and also that of the priestly class. *Carvaka* system worked out its philosophy in opposition to scriptural authority and other-worldliness. It is a materialistic philosophy that places most of its emphasis on the here and now of life as we perceive it and live through it. The *Carvaka* school accepts only empirical knowledge to be true and therefore dismisses the concept of afterlife. This school is, in fact, rejected by all other schools.

Indian psychology has developed around the existential quest to overcome human suffering, and in the process, help people to transcend to a higher level of psycho-spiritual existence. Thus, Indian psychology endeavours not only to provide an understanding of the nature of a person, the causes and consequences of his/her conduct, but also to explore the methods and means of transforming the person in pursuit of perfection, knowledge, and happiness. The basic inspiration behind each psycho-philosophical school has been to make the individual free from suffering and transcend to a higher level of existence. This notion that there is misery in this mundane world and one needs to transcend has percolated down to the folk level and is still widely believed in India. It may be added here that these are not just theoretical notions but are also accompanied by the social and personal practices to rise above the mundane.

Reincarnation of Indian Psychology

A new beginning of Indian psychology in present times can be traced in the writings of modern Indian sages, like Vivekananda,

Sri Aurobindo, Krishnamurthi and others in the last century. In the academic field number of publications were growing in which Indian theories were being discussed for their relevance in the present times. Some of this work is already discussed in the preceding sections. In the last two decades of the previous century, many important publications came out paving the way for reincarnation of Indian psychology in new form. Some of these publications are as follows: *Theoretical Psychology* (1984) and *Psychology of Self* (1998) by Paranjpe, *Consciousness Studies* (2002a) by Rao, *Handbook of Indian Psychology* (2008) by Rao, Paranjpe and Dalal, *Psychoanalysis and Indian Psychology* (2014) by Misra, and *Indian Psychology* (2015) by Rao and Paranjpe. Besides, a number of national conferences were held in Puducherry, Bangalore, and Delhi in the beginning of twenty-first century played an important role in putting Indian psychology on firm footing.

There is a visible change in attitude and perception of Indian psychology in last two to three decades. Indian psychology is growing in popularity among academic psychologists, as well among the practitioners, which is evident from the quantum of research and professional activities in this field.

By the turn of the millennium, the academic scenario is changing in India. The scientific community is better prepared now than in the past to accept a psychology rooted in native wisdom and philosophical texts. Psychologists in India are increasingly getting aware of the wide gap between their academic pursuits and the real-life problems of people. The recipient nature of research endeavours antiquated and obsolete teaching programmes, and lack of applied orientation have devoid the discipline of any professional momentum. Indian psychologists want to break free from the theoretical and methodological constraints of the discipline to grapple with the real issues of development and want to act as social catalysts in the change process. The endeavour is contemporizing Indian theories on one hand, and testing their relevance for enhancing human competencies and well-being, on the other. It is against this backdrop that Indian psychology is gearing itself to usher into a new era of exciting possibilities.

It is important that psychologists play an important role in rebuilding the nation. India's 85 per cent of the population is poor and 25–30 per cent of them are living in abject poverty. For many thousand years when science and philosophy was scaling new heights, Indian economy was also booming. We have to benefit from our past heritage and pick up the threads to speed up socio-economic development. We cannot revive our past in the present age, but can learn our lessons to balance inner development with material well-being. There is a need to engage in serious research at local as well as national level to carve out a role for Indian psychology for nation-building.

Features of Indian Psychology

Despite all diversity and distinctiveness there are some features which are common across all systems and schools relevant to Indian psychology. Some of these features, which give Indian psychology a distinct identity, are referred to in different sections of this book. These and other characteristic features of Indian psychology are discussed here in some detail.

Indian psychology is deemed to be a *universal science.* It deals with those principles which are cardinal to human life and are an integral part of their being. The origin of human being is considered essentially divine which oftentimes get contaminated by worldly experiences. This human temperament is fine combination of three components of *prakriti—satva, rajas,* and *tamas.* This temperament is given at the time of birth depending on one's past karma and manifest at different stages of life. The folk tradition is also not confined to the psychology of Indian people only. A vast body of research shows that many of the practices of natives or aboriginals, are common throughout the world, like not charging fee for health and healing services. Many of these practices are common in different regions because these have evolved on basic human psychology. Most of these theories are propounded as transhistorical, dealing with the intrinsic state and ways to enhance the human potential. It can be mentioned in this context that the teachings and training in Indian psychology are not intended for any particular class, caste, or creed, but people of all strata and culture can study and practice it (Radhakrishnan, 1953). Contrary to the misperception that traditional wisdom is accessible to the elite or Brahmins only, history is replete with instances in which many women and non-Brahmins have attained the highest level of knowledge. The declaration *aham bramhāsmi*

(I am *Brahman*) is followed by the phrase *tat tvam asi* (you are the same), which refers not only to all mankind but also to all living beings.

Two, Indian psychology primarily deals with the *inner functioning* of a person, taking consciousness as the primary subject matter of the study. Instead of emphasizing numerous contingent and non-contingent variations in acquired role-related behaviours the stress is on unchanging identity. In the *Upanishads,* consciousness as a state of being is not an object but is conceived as undifferentiated subjectivity (*chit*) without any content (Radhakrishnan, 1953). In the Indian tradition, consciousness happens to be the ground condition without which no reality is conceivable. It is the knowledge side of the universe, more than being a light source for apprehending sensations. The *Chandogya Upanishad* expounds four states of consciousness—waking, dream, deep sleep, and *turia* (illumined), the most desirable one being the last one. When the mind withdraws itself from participating in sensory processes by deliberate intent and empties itself of all content, it would be the illumined state of consciousness. When this happens, there arises unmediated direct knowledge characterizing *knowing by being* (Rao, 2005). It involves identity with existence and its knowledge. As the *Upanishadic* saying goes, 'to know *Brahman* is to be *Brahman*' (The *Mundaka Upanishad* III 3.2.9). Buddhism refers to the stream of consciousness as the basis of subjective feeling of continuity and identity which affects our perceptions, thoughts, actions, and emotion. While formulating five modes of knowing in Buddhism the focus has been on inner transformation, with the ultimate goal being liberation (Premasiri, 2008).

Sensory experiences leading to phenomenal awareness are intentional, that is, they focus on some objects of the world. Distortions in this case are due to active interference of mind and body, which limits our awareness, and obscures our knowledge and feelings. The goal of life is to attain a state of pure consciousness where knowledge is direct, immediate, and intuitive, and not mediated by sensory inputs which transform the person in totality and engages in a sincere seeking of higher-order truth. Transcendence and state of pure consciousness are held as attainable experiential realities, giving one a sense of freedom and liberation. Both transcendence and spirituality are aspects of the same reality and share this common pursuit. Spirituality furthers development of comprehensive theories of human existence to understand creativity, intuitive thinking, and extraordinary achievements (Bhawuk, 2003). Spirituality, however, goes with the sacred and the Divine, as Indian thought does not maintain any dichotomy between science and spirituality. They are grounded in the experiences of many and are attainable for anyone who follows systematic procedures and practices. Though transcendence and spirituality are at the core of most of the Indian theories, these are not bound by any particular faith or ism and serve to provide a secular account of human nature.

Indian psychology is an *applied science*. It is not just concerned about testing theoretical positions, or engaging in speculative metaphysical inquiry. It raises important questions about the ideal state of being and deals with the methods one can follow to attain that state. It discusses the practices through which people can transform their own lives to attain perfection, and thereby change the world they live in. The goal of Indian psychology is to help a person move from a conditioned state (mechanical and habitual thinking and responding) to an unconditioned state of freedom and liberation. This transformation, in more mundane terms, implies becoming more objective, discretionary, equipoise, and aware about the potential sources of distortion. Indian psychology extensively deals with the ways of handling human suffering and leads one on a path of growth, which does not create any hurdle for other co-travellers. The techniques of yoga and meditation have contributed significantly toward self-control of mind and feelings. Such techniques are diverse to suit people of various orientations. Thus, *bhakti* (devotion), *karma* (action), or *jnana* (knowledge leading to renunciation) yoga can be used by any person depending upon his or her temperament or dispositional orientation (*svabhāva*). The theories and practices of Āyurveda are fine examples of how the mundane can be blended with the transcendental.

It should not be misconstrued that Indian psychology is only concerned with inner transformation and does not deal with the mundane problems of this world. It has a vision of a social order in which conflict, violence, injustice, and exploitation have no place. It offers mechanisms to address the problems arising from human greed, attachment, and egotism, which culminate in poverty, injustice and pain. Indian psychology is equally concerned with the challenges of education, mental and physical health, and social institutions, and has offered alternative models and methods. Indian psychology does not dismiss the empirical approach in these areas but by being positioned at an appropriate level provides a broader perspective within which its findings would make sense.

Misconceptions and Criticisms

After introducing and elaborating what Indian psychology is, we are in a better position now to deal with misconceptions and criticisms about it. It is necessary to understand Indian psychology in the right context and not to be swayed by tall claims which its proponents keep making and its undue criticisms by detractors. Indian psychology is still finding its footholds as a scientific endeavour in the present times and such an ongoing debate about what it can accomplish is healthy for its growth.

Indian Psychology is a Prescriptive Science

All social and psychological theories are shaped in the cultural firmament. The values, priorities, and ethics of that culture provide the ingredients on which these theories are built and sustained. No social science can thus be prescription-free. Many of these prescriptions could be implicit in hypotheses, designs, and interpretations of the findings. For example, an innocuous experiment of Asch (1951) on social conformity, in which the effect of peer pressure upon modification and distortion of judgment on a perceptual task, was studied. Asch demonstrated that when there is group pressure (other members are deliberately making wrong judgments), the real subjects tend to distort their judgments. His work apart from demonstrating social conformity has a clear message that conformity is bad as it results in wrong judgments. Western theories are the product of a value system of individualism, capitalism, and materialism, whereas, in Indian psychology transcendence is the core value. Indian psychology which grew in a different historical and cultural milieu is also a prescriptive science, having a vision of an ideal society and an ideal person. Accordingly, the methods that are developed are also designed to attain that desirable state. Keeping that in view, Indian psychology is sacred and spiritual, and yet endorses a secular cultural ethos that highly values a transcendental state of being. The goal of Indian self-psychology is to examine one's state of consciousness and understand the metamorphosis that one goes through.

Notwithstanding, Indian psychology is as descriptive and confirmatory as any other social science could be. It has evolved as a well-laid out methodology to test and describe human conditions and conditioning. It has sophisticated theories of mind and consciousness that are based on intersubjective validations. The process of understanding the reality, which is not mediated by sensory inputs or the conditioned mind, gives rise to the ultimate knowledge. This knowledge transcends, according to Indian psychology, the prescriptive–descriptive dichotomy, as well as all language barriers, as one understands the truth at a direct intuitive and experiential level.

Indian Psychology is Faith Psychology

It is argued that science builds on doubting and questioning. It is part of the training of a scientist to be a sceptic and question the veracity of the existing findings, that is, not to accept anything unless it is empirically tested. Faith has no place in scientific diction, 'when you observe you trust'. Indian psychology takes a position that its reverse is also true: 'when you trust you observe'. For example, when you trust that there is an observer (*purusha)* inside you who is watching everything you tend to experience it. Similar is the case of the sixth sense; when you believe in its existence, then you notice it. This is how faith works.

Indian Psychology is Otherworldly

Indian psychology is not obsessed with otherworldly matters as it is often misunderstood. It does transcend the boundaries of the mundane and does not draw a rigid line between the physical and metaphysical. But still the life after life is not the subject matter of Indian psychology, nor is it a discourse on metaphysics. The primary focus is on how people can lead a purposeful and wholesome life. Both *parā vidyā* (knowledge of the self) and *aparā vidyā* (empirical knowledge) are considered necessary to live a harmonious life in this world. Even transcendence, which is often taken in an otherworldly sense, has worldly aspects. In mundane terms, it signifies transformation of an individual such that one is able to know the truth and become objective by freeing oneself from biases and mental conditioning. In this sense transcendence implies overcoming the existential constraints of one's mind-body complex (Rao, 2008). It is always considered possible to attain the highest state of consciousness (*turiā*) in this life itself.

Self-growth is a major objective of Indian psychology but not in an otherworldly sense. Indian psychology deals with existential issues here and now. A person should attain freedom and liberation by realizing one's true nature for living a highest quality of life in this world. Psychology recognizes that physical processes influence mental functions, but it also stresses that mental functions influence bodily processes. It emphasizes the integral connection between consciousness, mind, and body. Therefore, neurophysiological studies are not considered irrelevant to Indian psychology, but are regarded as insufficient to give us a complete understanding of human nature.

Indian Psychology is a Separate Branch of Psychology

It may be posited here that Indian psychology does not aspire to be a distinct branch of psychology like social, personality, and clinical. Confining Indian psychology to a specific content domain, will do injustice to its vast potential and may deprive it of its diversity and richness. Indian psychology covers the whole range of human possibilities and, therefore, as a school of thought, has relevance for all branches of psychology. It creates new possibilities of looking at the age-old human problems of social conflicts and violence, emotional and mental health, human greed, and need for individual growth.

Whither Indian Psychology

Indian psychology is as old as the Indian civilization but its history as a modern discipline is very short. The new beginning of Indian psychology in the modern times can be traced in the work of Swami Vivekananda, Ramana Maharishi, and Sri Aurobindo in the early part of the last century. Subsequently, the monumental work of Jadunath Sinha (1958) on Indian psychology, a compilation of psychological concepts and theories in scriptures and other ancient texts, laid its firm foundation. However, it took much longer time for Indian psychology research to build up. It is only in the last two to three decades or so that the research in this area has picked up momentum and many important publications have come out. Looking at the plethora of research and publication activities going on at present it is likely that Indian psychology will have a critical mass sooner than later. As discussed earlier, it is a misnomer that Western psychology is universal and Indian psychology is not. Indian psychology is neither competing nor striving to replace Western psychology as a universal science. It only intends to offer an alternative perspective. Whereas Western science has focussed on the human problems, Indian psychology primarily looks at the growth aspects, that is, on how human beings can actualize their full potential and can free themselves from their mental conditioning. In this sense, Western psychology and Indian psychology can complement each other by bringing the whole range of human possibilities into the fold of research. It is in this respect that Indian psychology claims its legitimate place as a global mainstream psychology.

However, despite all possibilities and provocations, Indian psychology is still struggling to make inroads into the academic citadels of Indian universities. There are only few departments where courses on Indian psychology are being taught, and there is still a good deal of resistance to introduction of Indian psychology into their teaching programmes. Ostensibly, a larger body of Indian psychologists is still wary of the nature and agenda of Indian psychology. There are wide ranges of apprehensions which have stalled the acceptance of a psychology of Indian origin. Some such apprehensions are briefly discussed here.

First, Indian theories of mind and consciousness are often held to be subjective and not amenable to scientific testing. Consequently, Indian psychology is not considered an appropriate discipline for empirical research using established scientific methodology. As such, Indian psychology is considered to be mostly speculative which may reduce the science of psychology to a non-scientific enterprise. Second, a majority of Indian psychologists are concerned about keeping pace with advancements in empirical research methodology and statistical techniques, which give psychology the status of a highly sophisticated scientific enterprise among all social sciences. Indian psychologists, primarily trained in positivistic methods, are more at ease in employing the methods of Western sciences. Third, scientifically minded psychologists still consider Indian psychology as part of a religious (worse, revivalist) movement. Many are of the view that the subject matter of Indian psychology is esoteric, mystical, and metaphysical. Therefore, there is an anxiety that including Indian psychology in the academic curriculum would undermine the secular credentials of their scientific pursuits; that such a move may offend the sensibilities of the scientists of other faiths. Fourth, working within the domain of Indian psychology will cut them off from the rest of the world and may label them as being parochial or ethnocentric. This may deprive their research of a wider transnational recognition and may foreclose the possibilities of international collaboration and support. In fact, many yoga research institutes, like Swami Vivekananda Yoga Kendra, Bangalore are getting international attention on par with the best research institutes in the world. Lastly, there is a practical reason for sticking to Western psychology in academia. There is no tangible incentive to the academic community to change their areas of specialization. It may be more rewarding to do research, for example, in the area of emotional intelligence than, say, on detachment. Indian psychologists require sustained efforts to re-educate themselves, which is hard put without peer support, reading material, and training programmes.

Nandy (1995) has argued that conducting experiments, developing and adapting psychological tests, and mindlessly replicating Western research is what has kept Indian psychologists occupied without any clarity of purpose. These Indian psychologists are often aware that the psychology they are pursuing does not address the real issues of change and development, both at social and individual level. They know that this will call for in-depth analysis of the socio-psychological problems of Indian society. A discontentment is brewing among the psychology fraternity about the state of psychology in India. An urgent need is felt to relook the processes of teaching, training, and research in psychology with an open mind and cultural sensibility. This asks for a paradigm change in psychological research in India.

One trend which is disturbing is about Indian psychology becoming part of popular but trivial research in academic educational institutions. A large number of tests and scales are developed to quantify Indian concepts, giving scant consideration to specific ontology and epistemology in which Indian concepts are embedded. These concepts cover larger terrain and it is doubtful whether or not these are amenable to measurement. Like, there are number of scales to measure three *gunas*, which is a way of trivializing value-loaded, complex cultural terms. Trying to straightjacket such complex Indian concepts without embedding them in some theoretical framework and then subjecting them to Western methodology may do more harm than good. There is vast research demonstrating that *nishkan* (detached) karma is a good strategy for marketing. Such research is dangerous and we need to be varying of this growing trend in social-science research.

Despite all resistance and setbacks, Indian psychology seems to be gathering momentum, if attendance at Indian psychology conferences, workshops, and research publications are taken as an indicator. There is a good deal of excitement and sense of purpose in a section of psychologists who are pursuing Indian psychology. It can be easily discerned that this newly emerging science of Indian psychology calls for a paradigm shift. We need a serious and sustained debate on nature, characteristics, and implications of this new paradigm. A dominant view is that the Western and the Indian paradigms are irreconcilable and cannot have a meeting ground. Indian concepts and theories are grounded in different notions of the human nature, epistemology, values, and worldview, than the Western ones. However, the range of problems the humanity is facing needs both the paradigms. Whereas the methodology of Western psychology focuses on the study of the 'other' person, Indian psychology (as other Eastern psychologies) focuses on the study of one's 'own-self'. We need both first-person and third-person approaches to bring about the desired changes in human condition. Indian psychology's experiential basis of knowledge generation is common to the theories and practices of many other Eastern philosophies, including Zen, Tao, and Buddhism. The proponents of this position hold that building a more harmonious and conflict-free world order, where people are able to actualize their inner potential, can be a valid goal. It is hoped that turning toward Indian psychology would help the discipline by expanding the scope of psychological inquiry and by offering technologies for self-transformation leading to a better quality of life.

Moreover, working in the field of Indian psychology needs a wider collaboration with scholars of Sanskrit, philosophy, Indology, and spiritual experts who can help in understanding Indian cultural theories and concepts to develop testable hypotheses. Majority of the academic psychologists have almost no training to comprehend finer nuances of the subject matter, and such collaborations are imperative. We need refinement of the age-old methodologies and innovation in developing new methodologies to test Indian concepts. This needs committed and concerted effort over longer period of time.

Again, Indian psychology has always been experiential and transformative. Apart from other things, research aims to change the researcher. We who are trained in the Western psychology, do not know how to handle this waxed issue. Focus of research on own-self has implications of different order for both researcher and for subject of research. Doing research on own-self needs a new paradigm and tools which need to be harnessed by the researcher. Using yoga as a research method to examine inner states is one such example. This is problematic as how can a mind study itself and thereby go beyond itself. Indian sages in olden times had mastered many techniques of yoga to examine the inner mechanism of life and living. In modern times we need to refine the earlier instruments and develop new ones to advance knowledge in the field of Indian psychology. This is obviously easier said than done.

We would not know if Indian psychology is a serious field of inquiry or turning into fad and fashion. Many contradictory trends are emerging which have made the whole situation rather confusing. If we appraise the trend of the last three decades we cannot reach to a conclusion. Three trends are emerging. One, Indian psychology is building up as a movement, slowly but perceptibly, if we see in terms of research productivity. The bulk of this research is of poor quality in national and local journals, and rarely of quality in international journals. It could be because of many reasons. There is a mushrooming growth of local journals in which all kinds of papers are published. According to UGC survey, 90 per cent of these journals (UGC, March 2018) are of very poor quality. They are rehashing of ancient Indian concept or are of survey type. It is observed that the quality of research has declined in India over the years and that is perceptible in the area of Indian psychology also. Two, after three decades of efforts, Indian psychology is taught only in two or three psychology departments across the country. Academic psychologists have not been able to develop expertise in this new field. They resist moving away from scientific Western psychology in which they are trained. Indian psychology cannot be taught purely as a classroom subject, as a study of self it has to be distinguished from other fields. There is no pedagogy developed to teach this new discipline now, nor is there any discussion at the national level. Even the new national curriculum brought out by UGC is primarily based on Sri Aurobindo's teaching and people from Ashram. Rao and Paranjpe are the only two prominent psychologists whose work is included. Such a casual approach is likely to do more harm than good to this budding new discipline. Three, Indian psychology does not fit in the prevailing academic culture of university departments. Adding one or two courses at undergraduate or postgraduate level is not likely to change the prevailing ethos, rather there are more chances that Indian psychology will get drafted in the prevailing mould and its uniqueness and impact will get lost.

There is an apprehension that Indian psychology may be hijacked by those for whom commercial interest is paramount. Anything which is labelled as Indian may sell potential and there is the research to suggest this. Research articles suggest that marketing products with *nisham*-karma approach augments its sale. There is research which shows that spirituality leads to greater commitment to work place and improves productivity. Such piecemeal research leads nowhere. Three or four decades is not a longer time to evaluate the progress of a discipline but there should be some markers of its progress. We still do not know where is Indian psychology heading. One can argue either way.

In psychology courses, Indian psychology and indigenous psychology should complement each other. As mentioned, one is the psychology of Indian people, whereas the other is universal psychology of Indian origin. Both psychologies taken should yield complete psychological profile of Indian people. We are yet to create a psychology which is relevant to human development and societal progress. The larger community of psychologists need to give a serious thought to train new generation of Indian psychologists for working in this field. One argument is to return to the age-old model of merging disciplinary interest to work together with other social sciences. A larger and cohesive vision is needed to plan projects in the area of Indian psychology, even moving out of the academic citadels to work with others who have practical experience.

2

The Core and Context of Indian Psychology

Indian psychology has its roots in the diverse traditions of knowledge deliberated upon in various texts (*Shastra*), as well as the practices, artifacts, and meanings embodied in various forms, shared by the people (*loka*) in the zone of Indian civilization. It is part of a living tradition which has continued unabated since time immemorial. As Thapar (2000) remarked, 'at certain levels there are aspects of cultural traditions in India that can be traced to roots as far back as a few thousand years' (p. xxv; Basham, 1954). Therefore, Indian psychology is different and broader than the academic psychology as it began in India in the beginning of the last century under the aegis of the scheme of Western domination. Indian psychology characterizes the Indian psychological viewpoints which are rooted in the Indian civilization. Indian psychology has evolved through rigorous observation, experimentation and reflection, through training under *gurus*, continuous contemplation, and sharing of personal accounts of inner

The earlier version of this chapter was published as 'Dalal, A.K. and Misra, G. (2010). Core and context of Indian psychology. *Psychology and Developing Societies*, 22(1), 157–91'.

experiences. This knowledge base has grown, diversified, and survived through many challenges and upheavals. It still continues, in a plural mode, to shape in explicit as well as implicit ways the dominant cultural ethos of the Indian people.

The thought systems and practices of Indian psychology, however, are pan-human in their basic conceptual orientation (Nakamura, 1964). Integrally bound with the Eastern philosophies, Indian psychology has evolved not as a moralistic but as a cultural discourse on worldviews and epistemologies, which offers an alternative to the logico-positivistic enterprise of Western psychology. Though originated in the Indian subcontinent, the concern has been to free human beings from bondages and suffering, wherever they are located and whatever their sources are. This discourse has grown around the essential nature of one's being and the various paths through which one comes to know about it. Indian psychology has endeavoured to create choices, finding out one's own *dharma* (duty) and pursue one's own path of evolution in a wider time–space framework. It situates human functioning in the cosmic context within which are embedded the personal, interpersonal, and communal-level engagements. Such ethos tend to promote democracy in ideas. It offers freedom to engage in diverse modes in a spirit of pluralistic enquiry and engagement. Indeed Indian psychology is built on the edifice of diverse schools of materialistic/realistic as well as idealistic thoughts. They offer disparate perspectives on understanding life and its potential for participatory growth and evolution in an interdependent world of existence. Menon (2005) takes the view that Indian psychology has expanded the conventional definition of psychology from the 'science of human behaviour' to 'human possibility and progress'. It has nurtured a worldview informed by continuity, interdependence, and connectivity across all life forms. It emphasizes an inclusive notion of field rather than individual as the centre of reality. The field (*kshetra*) and knower of the field (*kshetrajya*) are not mutually exclusive. By situating humans in a wider space–time continua this tradition offers a whole range of theories and concepts pregnant with many exciting hypotheses about human nature, their life course, and modalities of worldly engagements.

Indian sages and thinkers were struck by the immensity of the universe and the empirically inexhaustible mystery of life.

This wonder of existence is portrayed in the hymns of the *Vedas*, which attribute divinity to the striking aspects of nature (Radhakrishnan, 1953/1996) and the human mind (Sri Aurobindo, 1939/2006). In the Vedic texts it was held that the universe has evolved out of the *One*. This first principle of 'that One' (*tad ekam*) is considered uncharacterizable. It is without qualities or attributes, neither positive nor negative. Any attempt to describe it is to delimit and bind that which is limitless and unbounded. All gods and deities are of late or secondary origin (Nasadiya Sukta 10:129, *Ṛig Veda*). What is important here is the view that holds continuity (*avyaya bhava*) and complementarity in various forms or manifestations of reality. It leads one to perceive unity in diversity and seeing no contradiction between the opposites. Thus, though later thinkers derived their inspiration from the *Vedas*, they were open minded and exercised freedom to interpret and elaborate the text(s) in different ways. The *Upanishads* are not the thoughts of a single thinker; they evolved over a period of time through scholarly discourses and contemplation. In the *Upanishads* the interest shifted from objective to the subjective, from outside world to self in whose infinite depths the universe is reflected in its entirety. The *Upanishads* give in some details about the path of the inner ascent, the inward journey toward ultimate reality. The Upanishadic seers extended the tenets of spirituality to the utmost bounds of human existence. The diversity of ideas, concepts, and visions encapsulated in the verses of the *Upanishads* has inspired generations of thinkers and has laid the foundations of Indian psychology.

It may be mentioned in this context that the *Vedic* seers admitted in all humility that their proposition of the creation was only a surmise, for it is not possible to be sure of the events that occurred in the distant past. They also conceded that the perfect and absolute cannot be known through the imperfect human mind. What is known about life and existence is therefore conjectural, logical, and intuitive in most of the cases. Scepticism and questioning is very much built-in in the mode of inquiry in the *Ṛig Veda* itself. It is said of Indra, 'Of whom they ask, where is he? Of him indeed they also say, he is not.' (*Ṛig Veda* II, 12). Such doubts are frequently raised throughout the classical texts and subsequently a whole system of inquiry called the *nyāya* was developed to ensure errorless thinking. Systematic dialogue (*samvād*) has been a potent method of advancing understanding about life and the universe. In the case of testing premises about self and transcendental knowledge, self-verification by using first-person experiential methods, like meditation, was considered to be the best option. This tradition of questioning and free thinking provided impetus to Indian psychology for centuries, and with many ups and downs, and setbacks it kept prospering till the recent times. In what follows, we present a brief history of Indian psychology and then note the changing perceptions of Indian psychology. We trace the disciplinary contours of Indian psychology and note its distinguishing features. To clarify the nature of Indian psychology, we then discuss what is not the core of Indian psychology before concluding the paper.

Brief Historical Background

For the last 100 years of its existence the contents and practices of teaching–learning of psychology in India has been dominated by the Euro-American tradition. The first department of psychology established at Calcutta University in 1916 was a discipline imported from the West but was supposedly universal in contents and theories. This incarnation of psychology was imbued with a Western spirit of objective knowledge and scientific methodologies. Even after the political Independence of India in 1947, psychology continued to grow in the same institutional framework and learning paradigm, with its anchor deeply entrenched in behaviourist ideology. It has been alien in the sense that the teaching was primarily in terms of sharing and propagating the Euro-American principles and practices, rather than applying and linking to social reality with an open mind. Though it did expand rapidly in the Indian universities and institutes of higher learning and professional training, it mainly served the purpose of substantiating and illustrating the principles of Western scientific psychology taking Indian samples with little contribution to the (supposedly universal) body of knowledge pool called psychology. While some scholars did try to relate to Indian ethos and attended to explicate indigenous sources of knowledge they did that privately, and the public face projected in curriculum and teaching programme did not incorporate that as legitimate and worthwhile. The idea of psychology and its preferred way of categorization and conceptualization was held pre-cultural or a cultural, and culture was given no place in the constitution of psychological materials or elements. For example, motives, drives, needs, perceptual learning, and various cognitive phenomena were kept separate from the cultural tradition. The dynamics of creating a niche for a new discipline and the pressures to form identity amidst physical science disciplines might have led to this. By the mid-70s, discontentment was brewing among some Indian psychologists who cared for application and relevance of their efforts (Dalal, 1996). To the vast majority, a psychology patterned after physical science model was treated as intrinsically universal, in which there was no scope for Indian or for that matter any other non-Western perspective.

The trinity of materialism, quantification, and objectivity of Western psychology and commitment to the very goal of science to control and manipulate others fascinated Indian psychologists. This ethos of a new science of psychology was so captivating that most of the courses became immune to the cultural context. For instance, the courses offered at master's level had a compulsory component of history of psychology but they were silent about Indian contributions, nor was there any disciplinary engagement with Indian culture and society but British, Greek, European, and American philosophical contributions captured the entire space. Such a decontextualized training could survive merely on the ground of metatheoretical suppositions of the universality of the basic principles of psychology, its way of categorization and understanding. It subscribed to a mechanistic and reductionist framework supported by an empiricist methodology.

It may be noted that the growth of scientific psychology has resulted in losing the essential constituents, such as psyche and consciousness, and making the enterprise an empirical discipline, which is composed of things borrowed from various disciplines and nothing of its own. As such, psychology is so disintegrated and fragmented that a meaningful definition of the discipline is next to impossible. Today psychology is experiencing fragmentation and its diverse applications make it contingent on variable contexts (Misra and Kumar, 2008). The illusion of developing grand empirically derived theories and principles of human behaviour and action could not sustain for long. One finds distinct changes in the academic scenario in the field of psychology that have created avenues for an engagement with culture. The emergence of cross-cultural, ethno, indigenous, and cultural psychological approaches brought into focus the significance of culture in understanding psychological processes. Also, the supremacy of physical science as the prototype of inquiry into human affairs has been questioned by the philosophers of science (e.g. Derrida, 1982; Foucault, 1977; Gergen, 1989a). This has led to revision of the nature of understanding of science and scientific enterprise. A related development has been the increasing use of qualitative methods which rely on subjectivity, human experience, and a constructivist approach to human understanding. These developments facilitated the emergence of a critical look at the disciplinary affairs and various possibilities have emerged.

The realizations within the community of psychologists in India emanating from self-reflection and growing discomfort with the limitations of academic engagements within the received paradigm, at conceptual as well as societal planes, led to a nationwide reflection and debate among Indian psychologists. The result was a distinct clamour to indigenize the prevailing Euro-American discipline and made it culturally sensitive. Sinha (1965) gave a call for integration of modern psychology with Indian thought. Many significant works involving critique and reconstruction have come out in the following decades. Sinha's writings (1998, 1997, 1986, and 1981) persistently endeavoured to make the point that psychology has to be culturally relevant and called for indigenization of the discipline. A large number of publications have come out during this period critically reviewing the state of psychology in India and urging the colleagues to make it socially relevant and compatible with the Indian ethos (Dalal, 1996; Gergen et al., 1996; Misra and Gergen, 1993; Misra and Mohanty, 2002; Misra, Prakash, and Verma, 1999; Pandey, 2004, 2001; Sinha, 2000a; b). Amidst much confusion and lack of self-confidence, the move to articulate and nurture psychology with Indian concepts and theories took considerable time in gathering momentum. However, these efforts to rejuvenate psychology in the ancient texts intensified in the 80s and 90s. Some notable publications of this period are by Chakraborty (1995), Paranjpe (1998, 1984), Saraswathi (1999), and Rao (2005, 2002b, 1988). This stream has built not only on the interpretation of traditional concepts and theories in contemporary idiom, but also on their integration within a broader, global perspective. A comprehensive approach to Indian psychology involves issues of justice and *dana* (Krishnan, 2005); poverty (Misra and Tripathi, 2004); interpersonal relationship (Kakar and Kakar, 2007); organizational development (Singh–Sengupta, 2007); creativity (Bhawuk, 2003); concept of self (Bhawuk, 2005); pain and suffering (Anand, 2004, 2006); emotions and their effects (Bhawuk, 2008a; Jain, 2004; Misra, 2005, 2004; Paranjpe, 2009; Singh and Misra, 2005); religious behaviour and devotion (Paranjpe, 2007); and, peace and well-being (Bhawuk, 1999; Dalal and Misra, 2005; Kumar, 2004; Misra and Srivastava, 2004), to name just a few.

In more recent times, efforts to build Indian psychology as a vibrant discipline have intensified. Several conferences (Puducherry, 2001, 2002, 2004; Kollam, 2001; Delhi, 2002, 2003, 2007; Vishakhapatnam, 2002, 2003, 2006; Bengaluru, 2007) have given impetus to this movement of Indian psychology. The publication of the *Journal of Indian Psychology* since 1976, NAOP Conventions at Kanpur (2007) and Guwahati (2008), refresher courses in Indian psychology at Mysore, courses at Indian psychology Institute at Puducherry for the last four years, publications, such as Misra and Mohanty's *Perspectives on Indigenous Psychology* (2002), Joshi and Cornelissen's edited volume, *Consciousness, Indian Psychology and Yoga* (2004); Rao and Marwaha's *Towards a Spiritual Psychology* (2005); and Rao, Paranjpe, and Dalal's *Handbook of Indian Psychology* (2008) has made rich source material on Indian psychology available.

The newly emerging psychology is rooted in traditional Indian thoughts and practices that have existed at least for the last 2500 years as a holistic human science. The plurality of the Indian intellectual tradition and an ethos of accommodating diverse thought systems extend immense opportunity for creatively building a new psychology. As stated in the *Pondy manifesto* (2002), *Rich in content, sophisticated in its methods and valuable in its applied aspects, Indian psychology is pregnant with possibilities for the birth of new models in psychology that would have relevance not only for India but also for psychology in general.* This manifesto signed by the delegates at the Indian psychology conference at

Puducherry was a landmark event in the history of Indian psychology.

It needs to be made explicit that the purpose of identifying, developings, and testing Indian concepts and theories is not to prove their intrinsic superiority. It is a theoretical and methodological movement toward contemporizing Indian theories and testing their relevance for enhancing human potential, enhancing well-being, and making this world a better place to live. It is against this backdrop that Indian psychology is gearing itself to usher into a new era of many exciting possibilities.

The Changing Perceptions of Indian Psychology

Ostensibly, there is a change in attitude and perception of Indian psychology in the last decade or so. That Indian psychology is growing in popularity among academic psychologists, as well among practitioners is evident from the quantum of research and professional activities in this field. Three factors that have contributed to this change in attitudes toward and perceptions of Indian psychology are discussed herewith.

First, Western psychology has failed in dealing with the societal problems that are faced by the people in non-Western world. It has increasingly been realized that psychology driven by the positivist paradigm only provides a fragmented and superficial account of human feelings, behaviour, and the dynamics of action of an isolated individual (Nandy, 1988). The growing problems of social and family violence, mental ill health, moral decay, etc. have brought out the gross limitations of the mainstream Western psychology to the Western scholars as well. The concept of human being as an epicentre of the universe and container of myriads of psychological attributes (e.g. abilities, motives, interests, goals, dispositions, cognitions, and aptitudes) is flawed as it does not capture the totality of existential context of life. The principles thus derived were largely framed within a deficit model and ignored certain important and affirmative human phenomena (e.g. religion, spirituality, suffering, values, authenticity, creativity, love, collectivism, and forgiveness), which have emerged under the rubric of positive psychology (Snyder and Lopez, 2002). As a movement within positivistic epistemological tradition, positive psychology too is not equipped to handle inner, personal, cultural, and subjective aspects of life. These issues were either left unattended or appropriated in a trivial fashion that made them less appealing.

It is interesting to note that the limitations of the practices of positivist psychology were noted in the Western world too. For instance, Worchel and Cooper (1989) had discussed the crisis in modern social psychology and its limitations in dealing with the contemporary social problems. Humanistic and transpersonal movements in the 1960s were largely protest movements against scientism which is primarily concerned about control and prediction, ignoring phenomenological perspective in psychological research (Wertz, 1998). Modern psychotherapies too are going through a crisis of identity and a debate is raging about their goals, philosophy, and moral vision (Vanden Bos, 1996). A need is felt to bring back spirituality and religiosity in psychological research and theorization (Bhawuk, 2003), which was banished from psychology for about a century (see special issue of the *American Psychologist*, January 2004). All these contemporary developments are in response to the acutely felt limitations of psychology developed and practiced within the framework of modern science. Modelled on the mechanistic–reductionist paradigm of physical sciences, Western psychology is very restrictive in its assumptions about human nature and cannot deal with larger human concerns. A rethinking has led to emergence of new perspectives and paradigms in psychology (i.e. in terms of feminism, social constructionism, and postmodernism—Gergen 2007, 2009; Stanley, 1990), which in certain ways bridges the gap between Eastern and Western understanding of human nature.

Second, there is a growing popularity of yoga and other spiritual systems in the West. In the past few decades, more and more people with spiritual training and experiences from India have been visiting other countries and have acquired a large following. They have been responsible for disseminating the Indian spiritual tradition. Among them, Maharishi Mahesh Yogi and Swami Rama are prominent who have been able to draw the attention of academic psychologists. Sri Aurobindo's *Integral Yoga* and *Integral Psychology* have attracted worldwide attention (Sri Aurobindo, *The Integral Yoga, The Life Divine* in 2 volumes). Mahesh Yogi's Transcendental Meditation (TM) went through rigorous experimental testing at Harvard and other universities. Swami Rama offered himself to extensive medical testing at the

Menninger Foundation Laboratory, New York, where he demonstrated many yogic feats (Swami Rama, Ballentine, and Ajaya, 1976). These Indian masters were able to demonstrate convincingly the power of mind over body and have contributed significantly toward evoking interest in the explication of Indian perspectives. The presence of Ram Krishna Mission, Swami Narayan, Shivanand, Muktanand, Sikh saints, and many who settled in the West have also contributed to generate interest in Indian psychology. Publications of Sri Aurobindo Ashram, Puducherry, and the Himalayan International Institute for Yoga Sciences, Philosophy, and Religion in Honesdale, Pennsylvania, founded by Swami Rama, are valuable for their significant role in expounding the psychological insights of *vedanta, yoga, samkhya,* and other systems of Indian thought. These and many other accomplished spiritual masters of the Indian tradition have played an important role in popularizing Indian psychology across the globe (Paranjpe, 2006). Mahatma Gandhi's life and works have also inspired modern thinking on peace, development, and conflict resolution (Bondurant, 1965; Horsburgh, 1968; Pelton, 1974).

Though rooted in Indian scriptures and philosophical texts, Indian psychology does not promote any religious faith, nor is it based on any particular metaphysics; rather it has a quality that transcends all religious boundaries and does not offend any faith or ideology. Various schools of thought within the Indian system cover the whole range of theistic and atheistic (e.g. *sankhya* and *Charvak)* postulates of life. Also, Indian psychology has drawn not only from ideology and scriptures of Hinduism but also from other schools of thought, including Buddhism, Jainism, and Sufism. Yoga and meditation, for example, are not limited to any particular religious faith and can be tested and practiced by the people of all faiths anywhere. Indian psychology has much to offer in terms of self-growth, independent of any specific religious tradition. How to liberate human beings from the bondage of ignorance and suffering, and how to create a social order of harmony, peace, and personal growth constitute its major agenda. A human being in such a conceptualization is not merely an intelligent live structure interested in survival and self-growth. Instead he or she is an active and responsible part (or partner) of nature and its growth and survival are contingent upon the growth and survival of other co-inhabitants of this universe. To this end, one's consciousness operates as a great asset. In the West, interest in the study of altered states of consciousness since 1960s and the founding of transpersonal psychology as a sub-discipline encouraged psychologists to examine some of the indigenous perspectives. It was recognized clearly that Western psychology has nothing to offer regarding the spiritual/transcendental dimension of human nature, to understand others or for self-realization (Tart, 1975, 2009).

Third, with India emerging as a major economic power in the world, there is a renewed interest in Indian thought systems, values and practices, as well as in the strength and resilience of Indian society. Till the seventeenth and eighteenth centuries, when India was one of the richest countries in the world, European opinion about India was unequivocally positive. Indian philosophy, mysticism, art, and literature were looked upon with awe and appreciation. It was in the later period when Indian civilization was in decadence and became impoverished due to colonization, reducing India to one of the poorest countries, that the Western Indologists (McCaulay 1835/1972; James Mill[1], 1848) started debunking Indian culture and philosophy for India's poverty and backwardness. Western scholarship had unique reading of Indian culture that attributes India's underdevelopment to the lack of traits and characteristics found in the industrialized Western societies. Thus, low n-Ach (McClelland, 1961), dependence proneness (J.B.P. Sinha, 1970), hierarchy and relational orientation (Hofstede, 1980) were treated as negative attributes. Interestingly the situation has changed in recent years. The same Indian culture and its philosophy are now seen behind India's economic success. With Indian economy going from strength to strength and with the visibility of Indian IT professionals at strategic locations worldwide the attitudes and perceptions about the Indian way of thinking have changed (Varma, S., 2004). The number of courses taught in American and European universities on Indian culture, philosophy, spirituality, art, and music has increased significantly. Indian research acquired greater respectability and is now taken more seriously by the Western psychologists and as a consequence (ironically), by Indian psychologists themselves.

The Disciplinary Contours

What is *Indian* in Indian psychology? In terms of field, content, and methodology, Indian psychology maintains a distinct position, which differs from the widely held assumptions of Western psychology. Even when consciousness, mind, and intuition are included as the subject matter, Indian psychology stands as a body of knowledge rooted and pursued with different ontological and epistemological premises. More than materialistic–deterministic aspects of human existence, Indian psychology takes a more inclusive spiritual-growth perspective on human existence. In this sense no clear distinction is made between psychology, philosophy, and spirituality[2], as conjointly they constitute a comprehensive and practical knowledge or wisdom about human life. Another point to be noted is that Indian psychology has originated and prospered in the larger geographical region of Indian subcontinent and is compatible with the cultural and social life of the people; it has never been restricted to any given region. It fashioned itself on an existential plane which aspired for the upliftment of humanity in general instead of the people of Indian origin only. Indian psychology thrived on protest movements, like Buddhism and Jainism, and also on other philosophies of the region such as Zoroastrianism and Sufism. Its influence in the ancient times was far beyond the borders of greater India, Tibet, China, Japan, and Korea, and up to Sri Lanka, Malaysia, and Indonesia in the south, and to Afghanistan, Iran, and up to middle Asia in the West. Indian psychology was in communion with other contemporary philosophies of the East, such as Tao and Zen Buddhism, and this mutual influence is very much visible even today. They provided the intellectual and spiritual firmament to generate new ideas and explanations as evident in post-Upanishad texts (such as Shankar's non-dualism). Theories and practices of Indian psychology address wider existential issues and are relevant for the humanity at large in an inclusive manner. Though the term 'Indian psychology' implies a psychology of Indian origin, or a psychology that has grown in the Indian subcontinent, it functions at a level of abstraction which covers the humanity in general. It is only a coincidence that the term Indian psychology is used by the pioneers in this field, like

Jadunath Sinha who brought out three volumes entitled *Indian Psychology* (1933–58), Rhys Davids's book *The Birth of Indian Psychology and its Development in Buddhism* (1936), Raghunath Safaya's *Indian Psychology* (1975), and B. Kuppuswami's book *Elements of Ancient Indian Psychology* (1985). The latest in this sequel being the *Handbook of Indian Psychology*, edited volume by Rao, Paranjpe, and Dalal (2008). The term Indian psychology has thus come to stay.

Furthermore, as mentioned earlier, although no clear distinction was made between psychology and philosophy in the earlier times, Indian psychology is *psychology*, not just pure philosophical exposition of truth and intellectual debates. It is an applied and practical science which leads to testable hypotheses and experimentation aiming at inner transformation. As a science of a multilayered being, comprising of subtle inner being, physical being, and social being (Bhawuk, 2008a, 2005; Kumar, 2008), its propositions could not be tested by the accepted empirical methods of inquiry alone but require a broad spectrum of methodologies, calling for a wise and balanced deployment of first-person, second-person, and third-person perspectives (Bhawuk, 2008b). The process of knowing is informed by an encompassing worldview and pattern of social life weaved with the threads of the self and the sacred/divinity. From this vantage point, Indian psychology is a living science, formulated, tested, modified, and contextualized in the course of challenges encountered during struggles and tensions experienced in real life. It is an enterprise concerning spiritual development with rich epistemological tradition. It grew in tradition of critical examination where scholars and sages continuously proposed, analysed, interpreted, refined, and transmitted knowledge to the worthy disciples. It is remarkable that these institutions survived all along the history without much state support. Apparently Indian psychology is a complex field of knowledge comprising philosophy *(darshana),* life science (*āyurveda*), principles of personal and social conduct (*dharma shāstra, neeti, artha shāstra, kāma shāstra*), spirituality (*ādhyātma vidyā*), Jain and Buddhist scriptures, and texts of various socio-spiritual movements. The Muslim influence, particularly that of Sufism and Bahai, is also visible.

After centuries of unabated growth the new educational policy in British India in the nineteenth century brought forth a wholesale replacement of Indian 'knowledge culture' by the Western counterparts, in the field of education particularly (see Dharampal, 2000). When universities were established in India on the British pattern, the concerns and contents of Indian psychology survived in some of the philosophy departments. As long as philosophy and psychology were considered two sides of the same quest, there were philosophy departments where psychologists could possibly have access to the Indian tradition. But in the late 1950s when philosophy and psychology departments separated in Indian universities, psychologists turned en-mass toward Freud and behaviourism, and even this weak link was severed. Psychology as a discipline confined itself to the analysis of the visible world of concrete behaviour like any static, non-living physical object that can be measured and manipulated without any resistance.

The endogenous psychology, which underlines the contemporary relevance of cultural heritage and native theories, is what constitutes 'Indian psychology'. The plurality of Indian tradition and an ethos of accommodating diverse thought systems (e.g. Vedānt, Sāmkhya, Yoga, Āyurveda, Mimānsa, Jainism, Buddhism, Sufism, and Sikhism) offer a gold mine for building a more comprehensive and efficacious psychology. The precepts of Indian psychology encompass the entire range of human concerns and it is not possible to enumerate all of them here. However, as a point of departure from the accepted Western framework it seems in order to briefly mention a select few of them.

1. The four *purusharthas* (life pursuits), which are *dharma* (virtues and rightful obligations/duty), *artha* (material prosperity), *kāma* (fulfillment of desires), and *moksha* (liberation) cover the entire range of human possibilities and strivings, irrespective of caste, creed, or religion. For a happy and fulfilling life, these strivings should be pursued in harmony with *dharma* (social ethos). To this end it is held that the pursuit of goals like *artha* and *kāma* have to be made compatible with the requirements of *dharma*. Also, the idea of equanimity with respect to life experiences, positive or

negative, is a major learning in the *Bhagvad-Gitā*. Attachment with worldly objects and experiences are purely temporary and are of binding nature. Attachment to them ultimately destroys one's life. The *Bhagavad Gita* draws a temporal sequence of mental events as the following: Attachment → Desire → Anger → Mindlessness → Loss of memory → Loss of life (see Bhawuk, 1999, and also in this issue for a psychological model that captures these ideas).

2. It studies consciousness in its multifaceted manifestations and retains the core identity as a basic attribute. It recognizes multilayered existence (*panch koshas*) of human being, which has the potential to evolve and move toward higher levels of existence. The mere physical level (*ānnamaya kosha*) is the lowest level, and gradually through other levels *prānamaya*, *manomaya*, *vijñanmaya*, it goes to the level of *ānandamaya kosha*. The true identity (ātman) of *sat-chit-ānand* entails the highest level of existence (see Bhawuk 2008a for a synthesis of *pancha kosha* and physical, social, and metaphysical self). The contingent and acquired identities/superimposed attributes (*upādhis*) need not be confused with the core identity (*atman*) which remains unaffected and functions as a witness *(sākshi) (see Shankara in Vivekchudamani*, verse 501). This is the reason why there has been an emphasis on wise discrimination between permanent and impermanent (*nityanitya viveka*). The apparent existence is often considered as an illusion (māyā/prakriti) within which normal life is carried. It is the manifestation of the *ātman* that is often given independent and greater significance than *ātman* because of misunderstanding (*avidyā*). This *avidyā* is the main cause of attachments and consequent suffering. The existence of the same *ātman* in every human being offers a new way to see the prospects of humanity that deemphasizes the differences and draws attention to the intrinsic oneness of the humanity. It furnishes a rich ground for a spiritual psychology with *jiva* (embodied *ātman*) as the functioning unit. Its deliberations aim at developing principles that transform human beings for higher level of evolution.

The purpose of knowledge in traditional terminology, therefore, is liberation (*mukti*) from various attachments and overcoming the various kinds of suffering (*kleshas*) and ignorance. This, however, is not 'otherworldly' as the ideal personhood is to be *jivanmukta*—living a life with liberation. Expansion of identity for making it more encompassing and inclusive is the core of learning in this thinking. This implies that one must transcend the boundaries of ego since ego is not the real/true identity of a person. Coming out of the grips of egoistic attachments and engaging with non-egoistic or spiritual pursuits is a proposition, which is worth considering in the context of global challenge of sustainable development. Indian classical theories provide insight into the crisis caused by competition, consumerism, and selfishness.

3. Indian psychology recognizes the interplay of the manifest and unmanifest parts of our existence in shaping the events in this world. This makes room for going beyond strict determinism, accepting the emergent nature of reality. It suggests plausible explanations and strategies to deal with uncertainty. An important illustration of this is found in terms of classification of human action (*karma*) in terms of accumulated (*sanchit*) and in-action (*prārabdha*) *karma*. This classification implies that human action/behaviour is an evolving process, one that unfolds in the course of time. Also important is the idea of distributed notion of locus of control. Indian psychology has also expanded the notion of causality beyond self and non-self (internal–external) categories of perceived causes. Any action depends on the contribution of five factors, that is, *kartā* (agent), *karma* (action), *adhisthāna* (body), *karana* (instruments), and *daivam (providence)*—*The Bhagavad Gitā* (Ch. 18.14). The actor is one of them and contributes just a part of the total. This is in contrast to the usual categories of internal and external attribution, which lies within the domain of egoistic self.
4. Indian psychology emphasizes an organic view often explained in terms of the metaphor of seed and tree. This implies that continuity and transformation are inherent characteristics of life processes. In a major departure from linear mode of thinking, this metaphor underlines nonlinear

or cyclical mode of life functioning. It also implies the significance of the unmanifest in shaping one's life.

5. The human experience is complex and its study requires multiple methods including the third-person, second-person, and first-person methods. Indian psychology is not opposed to empirical methods as *pratyaksha* (perception) is one method (*pramāna*) accepted by all the schools of Indian thought but it is certainly not sufficient, particularly when we aim at both *parā* (self) and *aparā* (empirical) *vidyas* (knowledge). Being and knowing become, one once we venture toward transcendental realm. The empirical methods are not enough to address the entire range of human experiences.
6. Indian psychology does not view human action as neutral, value free, or a-moral. Instead it brings out the essential interdependence and interconnectedness of the worlds of human experience in which human beings are responsible players. At one level, it proclaims essential unity and asserts that self and non-self are identical in their constitution (i.e. *yat pinde tad brahmande*). This expands the scope of a discourse on human action.
7. While explaining human action, Indian psychology takes into account not only the actor but also the linkages among the person, time, and place. With emphasis on space (*dèsh*), time (*kāl*), and participant/person (*pātra*), it recognizes the nonlinear and emergent nature of action that defies simple descriptions in terms of binary categories of cause and effect (e.g. independent and dependent variables, predictors, and criterion). It is largely discursive and narrative, and cannot be reduced to simple binary categories. It is supplemented by the position taken by one Indian school of thought that assumes continuity between cause and effect (*satkarya vada*). It is reflected in the principle of karma held by a vast majority of the Indians that refers to the sequence of actions constituting cause and effect. Thus, actions necessarily entail certain consequences. This scheme also empowers the actor to shape the future course of events by engaging in a responsible action. One lives life in obligational relationship (*ṛinās*) with (*guru, ṛish, pitri,* and *bhuta*). Life, therefore, is a kind of sacrifice (*yajna*), a sacrifice of one's desires and ego.

8. Instead of merely describing reality, Indian psychology emphasizes on and promotes self-positive qualities through personal training and practice. The goal of such training is to nurture a balanced personality, which primarily involves *sātvik, rājasic,* and *tāmsik gunas* or qualities. Interestingly enough the objects in the surrounding environment also share these three properties and finally to transcend them. Therefore, the lifestyle should involve a harmonious relationship with one's environment and not by subjugating the environment. Such a relationship is mutually supportive for person and environment and does not tax any one of them. The *Āyurveda* talks of this harmony at the level of diet, action, and leisure to maintain health. Health is a state of balance (*samatva*) and a healthy person is one who is self-anchored (*swastha*) in a world of flux *(samsār)* with a body (*sharira*) that decays. It must be noted that while everyone has all the three *Gunas*, they exist in different combinations leading to a state of (im)balance reflected in the choice of actions and ensuring the health of mind, body, and spirit. A distinction has also been made between godlike and demonic qualities (*daivi* and *asuri sampat*) and it is recommended to evolve in the direction of godlike qualities. One's well-being requires adhering to a personal and social conduct rooted in virtuous life (*sukhasya mulah dharmah*—Chanakya.
9. The aspiration for transcendental existence helps overcome the body-centred egoistic strivings and offers a decentred view of self. It has implications for work and social relationship. It allows one to be motivated to treat work as a natural duty (*dharma*) to be performed with reference to the demands of the location in one's life space rather than any extrinsic incentive. It is one's humble contribution to the worldly operations. Instead of emphasizing on the outcome or reward outside the work context, this kind of thinking promotes competence in action as yoga (*yogah karmasu kaushalam*). Such competence requires sustained and detached action (*anasakti*). As indicated earlier, any action is made possible by several factors therefore attributing causality to self is ignorance. A person is a mere instrument

(*nimitta*) of divinity and, therefore, it is heightened egotism, which assigns personal causality.

Some Distinguishing Features of Indian Psychology

Despite all diversity and distinctiveness, there are some features common across all systems and schools relevant to Indian psychology. Some of these common features, which give Indian psychology a distinct identity, are briefly discussed in the following.

Indian psychology is deemed to be a *universal psychology*. It cannot be subsumed under the labels of indigenous, folk, or cultural psychology, if that purports to delimit the scope of psychological inquiry. For want of a new term it has been also labeled as *Greater Psychology* (Dalal, 2000). The vast expanse of Indian psychology attends to the perennial issues of human existence (e.g. bliss, conflict, happiness, health, human conduct, human strivings, justice, *kleshas*, meditation, misery, morality, pain, self-control, self-understanding, virtues, well-being, and yoga) which are not bound by any geographical region or time period. Centuries back the sages and thinkers were raising questions and attempted to address problems that are pertinent even today. In this sense, Indian psychology is both ancient and contemporary at the same time. Indeed, the use of the term 'Indian psychology' is more of a convenience; may be a more appropriate term is 'psychology of Indian origin' (Rao, 2008). While the roots of Indian psychology are decidedly Indian, it was never proposed as the psychology of Indian people. For instance, Buddhist psychology[3] is an integral part of Indian psychology, which flourished in Sri Lanka, Tibet, and Japan among other countries. Most of these theories are propounded as transhistorical, dealing with the intrinsic state and ways to enhance the human potential. It can be mentioned in this context that the teachings and training in Indian psychology are not intended for any particular class, caste, or creed, but people from all strata of the society can make themselves worthy of these pursuits (Radhakrishnan, 1953). Contrary to the misperception that traditional wisdom is accessible to men or Brahmins only, many women and non-Brahmins have attained the highest level of knowledge. The declaration '*aham bramhāsmi*' (*I am Brahman*) is always followed by the phrase '*tat tvam asi*' (you are the same), which refers not only to all mankind but also to all living beings.

Another important feature of Indian psychology is that it primarily deals with the *inner states* of a person, taking consciousness as the primary subject matter of study. Instead of emphasizing numerous contingent and non-contingent variations in acquired role-related behaviours, the stress is on unchanging identity. In the *Upanishads*, consciousness as a state of being is not an object but is conceived as undifferentiated subjectivity (*chit*) without any content (Radhakrishnan, 1953). In the Indian tradition, consciousness happens to be the ground condition without which no reality is conceivable. It is the knowledge side of the universe, more than being a light source for apprehending sensations. The *Chandogya Upanishad* expounds four states of consciousness—waking, dream, deep sleep, and illumined (*turia*); the most desirable one being the last one. When the mind withdraws itself from participation in sensory processes by deliberate intent and empties itself of all content, it would be the illumined state of consciousness. When this happens, there arises unmediated direct knowledge, characterizing *knowing by being* (Rao, 2005). It involves identity with existence and its knowledge. As the *Upanishadic* saying goes, 'to know *Brahman* is to be *Brahman*' (*The Mundaka Upanishad* III 3.2.9). Buddhism refers to the stream of consciousness as the basis of subjective feeling of continuity and identity which affects our perceptions, thoughts, actions, and emotion. While formulating five modes of knowing in Buddhism, the focus has been on inner transformation with the ultimate goal being liberation (Premasiri, 2008). The five modes of knowing are sensory, extra-sensory, holistic, insightful, and ethical. According to Buddhism, the knowing should not be based on authority, faith, belief, or speculation, but on personal experience.

Sensory experiences leading to phenomenal awareness are intentional, that is, they are of objects. Distortions in this case are due to active interference of mind and body, which limits our awareness, and obscures our knowledge and feelings. The goal of life is to attain a state of pure consciousness where knowledge is direct, immediate, and intuitive, and not mediated by sensory inputs. Human consciousness is considered hierarchical, the highest state being that of truth, pure consciousness, and bliss (*sat, chit,* and *anand*). Yoga and meditation are the processes for movement toward this transcendental state of pure consciousness. The engagement with pure consciousness makes Indian psychology transcendental in its orientation. Transcendence is a movement from mundane to sublime, from sensory to intuitive and from self (ego) to Self (enlightened). It is a psychological process of rising from narrow, personal reference of a problem that causes suffering to a transpersonal, holistic understanding, wherein the problem loses its sting. The transcendental view implies a position of self (ego) decentring and taking into consideration the whole range of progression in past, present, and future. It draws attention to non-egoistic and non-body centred encompassing vision of life and its processes. It enlarges or expands one's identity to incorporate others or anything or everything that exists (Self or all-encompassing Brahman!). The Upanishadic Mahavakyas (great sentences) like *Aham Brahmasmi* (I am *Brahman*) or *Sarvam khalvidam Brahman* (Everything is only *Brahman*) emphasize the value of ever expanding and inclusive identity. It sets the stage of an evolutionary journey in which the division of self and other or I/Me and you/they becomes meaningless as there is no other except one single I or Brahman. Transcendence, therefore, transforms the person in totality and engages in a sincere seeking of higher order truth. Transcendence and state of pure consciousness are held as attainable experiential realities, giving one a sense of freedom and liberation. Both transcendence and spirituality are aspects of the same reality and share this common pursuit. Spirituality furthers development of comprehensive theories of human existence to understand creativity, intuitive thinking, and extraordinary achievements (Bhawuk, 2003). Spirituality however goes with the sacred and divine, as Indian thought does not maintain any dichotomy between science and spirituality. They are grounded in the experiences of many, and are attainable for anyone who follows systematic procedures and practices. Though transcendence and spirituality are at the core of most of the Indian theories, these are not bound by any particular faith or ism, and serve to provide a secular account of human nature.

Indian psychology is based on *veridical* methods. It should be clear that as a human science of consciousness its methods ought to be different from the methods of natural/physical/material sciences. This, however, does not make it a less stringent science. Methods of observation and experimentation have also evolved to study the inner functioning of a person. In these methods of self-observation, no distinction is made between experience and observation, where true knowledge is not considered as abstract and impersonal but as realization of one's being (Rao, 2008). There are methods of direct observation (e.g. intuition) in contrast to methods that rely on sensory and mental mediation. These methods rely on the blending of first-person and second-person perspectives (collective). Taken together, these two perspectives allow personal, subjective and non-relational verification, and in-group inter-subjective validity. These methods work well, within *guru* (second person)–*shishya* or pupil (first person) methodologies.

Needless to say, the methods of yoga and meditation have been used for centuries to test and experiment, and for experiential validation of the higher mental states. The various systems of yoga in India have developed rigorous and effective methods of enquiry in the domains of consciousness studies and psychology that may help us to find answers to our deepest questions regarding values, truth, love, meaning, and beauty. They can offer to modern science not only a wealth of philosophical and psychological theories, but also a rich store of practical techniques to raise our individual and collective levels of consciousness.

It is relevant to mention here that in the Indian tradition a distinction is made between *parā vidya* (knowledge of the self) and *aparā vidya* (empirical knowledge). *Aparā vidya* constitutes the knowledge of social–physical world we live in and includes science and technology. This knowledge is also relevant to the problems and challenges of the world we live in. The methods of knowing in the empirical world (*pramāna*) are diverse and treat mind (*mānas* or *antahkaran*) as one sensory channel, which allows the understanding of pleasure and pain. They include methods such as perception (*pratyksha*), inference (a*numāna*), comparison (*upamāna*), verbal testimony (*sabda*), attribution of meaning (*arthapatti*), and historicity (*aitihya*). The system of Vedanta proposes methods of *sravana, manana*, and *nididhyāsana,* which correspond to sense-based knowledge, intellect-based knowledge, and intuitive knowledge, respectively (Rao, 2008).

Indian psychology is *applied* in its nature and objectives. It is not just concerned about testing theoretical positions, or engaging in speculative metaphysical inquiry. It raises important questions about the ideal state of being and deals with the methods one can follow to attain that state. It discusses the practices through which people can transform their own lives to attain perfection, and thereby change the world they live in. The goal of Indian psychology is to help a person move from a conditioned state (mechanical and habitual thinking and responding) to an unconditioned state of freedom and liberation. This transformation, in more mundane terms, implies becoming more objective, discretionary, equipoise, and aware about the potential sources of distortion. Indian psychology extensively deals with the ways of handling human suffering and leads one on a path of growth, which does not create any hurdle for other co-travelers. The techniques of yoga and meditation have contributed significantly toward self-control of mind and feelings. Such techniques are diverse to suit people of various orientations. Thus, *bhakti* (devotion), *karma* (action) or *jnana* (knowledge leading to renunciation) yoga can be used by any person depending upon his or her temperament or dispositional orientation (*svabhāva*; see Bhawuk's article on methodology in this issue). The theories and practices of Āyurveda are fine examples of how the mundane can be blended with the transcendental. The plurality in constitution, action and context is enunciated with the help of the theory of *trigunas* of *sattva*, *rajas*, and *tamas*.

However, it should not be misconstrued that Indian psychology is only concerned with inner transformation and does not deal with the mundane problems of this world. It has a vision of a social order in which conflict, violence, injustice, and exploitation have no place. It offers mechanisms to address the problems arising from human greed, attachment, and egotism, which culminate in poverty, injustice, and pain. Indian psychology is equally concerned with the challenges of education, mental and physical health, and social institutions and has offered alternative models and methods. Indian psychology does not dismiss the empirical approach in these areas but by being positioned at an appropriate level provides a broader perspective within which its findings would make sense.

What is *Not* the Core of Indian Psychology?

Indigenous psychological knowledge has a long traditional identity as an independent field of inquiry. As mentioned earlier, though there were writings in this area for many decades, it has emerged as a domain of serious research in academia only in the last one decade or so. We still do not have any critical historical document about the beginning and growth of Indian psychology. In this backdrop it is quite natural to encounter many misconceptions about what Indian psychology stands for, or does *not* stand for. To define Indian psychology as psychological knowledge rooted in Indian cultural heritage and scriptures dating back to more than three millennia and relevant to the contemporary world is not enough. As a growing science of Indian origin, Indian psychology is often held as a conglomeration of several, sometimes even contradictory fields of investigation. Indian psychology maintains its distinct assumptions about ontology, epistemology, and content. To arrive at some clarity about the subject matter of Indian psychology there is a need to engage in a dialogue about 'what constitutes Indian psychology and what does not'. We have already discussed what Indian psychology is; next we propose to discuss what Indian psychology possibly is not.

Indian Psychology is not just a psychology of Indian People

Due to common historical, social, and cultural background, it is natural that Indians share many dispositional and behavioural characteristics. On the very grounds, Indians would differ from Americans, Chinese, or any other ethnic group. Study of these cultural differences has been a very productive area of research in cross-cultural psychology. Being primarily a methodological field, cross-cultural psychology has taken the *etic* approach to establish equivalence of psychological phenomena for cross-cultural comparisons (Berry, 1989). On the other side, there is the *emic* approach which is employed when culture-specific phenomenon are investigated. Gergen et al. (1996, p. 501) stated, 'Cross-cultural psychologists were unable to abandon mainstream scientism in general and remain loyal to empiricism and test Western theories with "culturally" (i.e. geographically) diverse data'.

Both cross-cultural psychology and cultural psychology have examined how Indians differ from other cultural groups. The findings are often empirical generalizations and tend to make sweeping statements about the populations under investigation. Given India's vast ethnic diversity, these studies often fail to unravel enduring patterns and differences. Such research often ends up creating stereotypes about cultural groups. A good example is the debate about collectivism–individualism, in which countries are put in these two dichotomous categories (Triandis, 1984). As J.B.P. Sinha (2000a) argued, individualism–collectivism is a matter of sampling situations or persons and involves coexisting orientations (Sinha and Tripathi, 1994). In the absence of theoretical advancement and cultural constructs to interpret the results such findings often remain tentative. Making such comparisons and cataloguing psychosocial, emotional, and dispositional characteristics of the Indians have been attempted in many studies. Kakar's work on Indian psyche (1999, Kakar and Kakar, 2007) is a case in point in which the psychoanalytic framework has been used to interpret the findings. Such studies are at best tentative—interpretable only within a space–time matrix. On the other hand, Indian psychology endeavours to identify enduring human attributes and help people discover their essential nature and their relationship with the transcendental. Indian psychology strives to unravel atemporal and transcultural models of human ontology.

Indian Psychology is not Indigenous Psychology

D. Sinha (1994) has reminded us about two types of indigenization. The first is an outcome of adaptation of the mainstream (Western) psychology to a different cultural setup. This adaptation is along the lines argued by John Adair (1989). A large body of research in India can be included in this kind of indigenization in which cultural concepts and practices are examined employing Western theories and approaches. A large number of Western tests of personality, intelligence, motives, values, health, and well-being are indigenized taking this approach. Such indigenization is likely to continue in a global world where there is a constant flow of models and concepts across cultures, particularly from the West. The other kind of indigenization is that which is based on a systematic analysis of culture-bound concepts and categories. Such indigenization focuses on the contemporary relevance of cultural heritage and native theories which comes within the rubric of 'Indian psychology'. Misra and Mohanty's volume (2002) *Perspectives on Indigenous Psychology* includes Indian research that belongs to both the categories. Srivastava and Misra (2003) have undertaken the study of intelligence which is an example of the second kind of indigenization. They use multiple sources, that is, traditional texts, popular idioms, and layman's understanding and usage to develop a new model of intelligence. Indigenous psychology, in this sense, is synonymous to folk psychology, a disciplinary knowledge that has evolved in a particular societal context, which is used by laypeople to organize the conduct of their lives (George, 1999).

Many psychologists believe that *indigenous psychology* is a more apt term in this context. The plural term takes in its fold tribal, subaltern, and other communities that differ in their history, beliefs and social practices. Indigenous psychologies offer models and theories that can enrich our understanding of human psychology across cultures. Not acknowledging it, is akin to conceding to the position of Western psychologists that only they are developing universal theories, others are special cases of their theories. Indian psychology is more than such indigenous (or folk) psychologies for the reason that it offers psychological models and theories, derived from classical Indian thought, that hold a promise of panhuman interest.

Indian Psychology is not Faith Psychology

It is argued that science builds on doubting and questioning. It is part of the training of a scientist to be a sceptic and question the veracity of the existing findings, that is, not to accept anything unless it is empirically tested. Faith has no place in scientific diction, 'when you observe you trust'. Indian psychology takes a position that its reverse is also true: 'when you trust you observe'. For example, when you trust that there is an observer (*purusha*) inside you who is watching everything you tend to experience it.

Similar is the case of the sixth sense; when you believe in its existence, then you notice it. This is how faith works.

It can be argued that all scientific theories have some basic assumptions at the core. There is no inquiry that is not based on some assumptions. Western science (psychology in particular) has also built on a long tradition of socio-religious beliefs and practices. These assumptions are never questioned but without understanding them many theories would make no sense. For example, hedonism (that man seeks pleasure and avoids pain) is at the core of many social learning theories. Any assumptions can be held as a statement of faith and the two terms have the same connotation for research. Assumptions lead to metaphors, which determine the methodology to be employed and conclusions to be drawn. The behaviouristic psychology considered man as a machine, which suited its mechanistic models of learning and behaviour. The metaphor of the 'man as computer' changed the concerns and methodology of research, taking the human being as information processor. Similarly, the 'man as soul' metaphor holds human being as capable of rising above their physical limitations and attaining their transcendental state. Within this framework, the *Bhagavad Gita* propositions based on this metaphor in Indian psychology should be testable and experientially verifiable. The 'man as soul' metaphor calls for a different ontological and epistemological position in formulation of research questions but it certainly does not render Indian psychology as faith psychology.

Indian Psychology is not Otherworldly

Indian psychology is not obsessed with otherworldly matters as it is often misunderstood. It does transcend the boundaries of the mundane and does not draw a rigid line between the physical and metaphysical. But still the life after life is not the subject matter of Indian psychology, nor is it a discourse on metaphysics. The primary focus is on how people can lead a purposeful and wholesome life. Both *parā vidyā* (knowledge of the self) and *aparā vidyā* (empirical knowledge) are considered necessary to live a harmonious life in this world. Even transcendence, which is often taken in an otherworldly sense, has worldly aspects. In mundane terms it signifies transformation of an individual such that one is able to know the truth, and become objective by freeing oneself from biases and mental conditioning. In this sense transcendence implies overcoming the existential constraints of one's mind–body complex (Rao, 2008). It is always considered possible to attain the highest state of consciousness (*turiā*) in this life itself.

Self-growth is a major objective of Indian psychology but not in an otherworldly sense. Indian psychology deals with existential issues here and now even though it sees the relevance of the past experience for the present condition and the consequences of the present situation for the future, keeping open all possibilities without foreclosing any in haste. Indian psychology recognizes that physical processes influence mental functions, but it also stresses that mental functions influence bodily processes. It emphasizes the integral connection between consciousness, mind, and body. Therefore, neurophysiological studies are not considered irrelevant to Indian psychology, but are regarded as insufficient to give us a complete understanding of human nature.

Indian Psychology is not a Prescriptive Science

All social and psychological theories are shaped by the cultural firmament. The values, priorities, and ethics of that culture provide the ingredients on which these theories are built and sustained. No social science can thus be prescription-free. Many of these prescriptions could be implicit in hypotheses, designs, and interpretations of the findings. For example, an innocuous experiment of Asch (1951) on social conformity in which the effect of peer pressure upon modification and distortion of judgment on a perceptual task was studied. Asch demonstrated that when there is group pressure (other members are deliberately making wrong judgments), the subject tends to make distorted judgments. His work, apart from demonstrating social conformity, has a clear message that conformity is bad as it results in wrong judgments. Western theories are the product of a value system of individualism, capitalism, and materialism, as Indian psychology is a product of Indian value system of idealizing another social order. Indian psychology which grew in a different historical and cultural context is also a prescriptive science, having a vision of an ideal society and an ideal person. Accordingly, the methods that are developed are also designed to attain that desirable state. Keeping that in view, Indian psychology is sacred and spiritual, yet endorses secular cultural ethos that highly value a transcendental state of being. The goal of Indian self-psychology is to examine one's state of consciousness and understand the metamorphosis that one goes through.

Notwithstanding, Indian psychology is as descriptive and confirmatory as any other social science could be. It has evolved a well laid out methodology to test and describe human conditions and conditioning. It has sophisticated theories of mind and consciousness that are based on intersubjective validations. The process of understanding the reality, which is not mediated by sensory inputs or the conditioned mind, gives rise to the ultimate knowledge. This knowledge transcends, according to Indian psychology, the prescriptive–descriptive dichotomy, as well as all language barriers, as one understands the truth at a direct intuitive and experiential level.

Indian Psychology is not Just a Study of Ancient Wisdom

Indian psychology is not merely a historical documentation of the ancient Indian wisdom. Scriptures dating back thousands of years are, of course, a vast treasure house of wisdom that has remained hidden and inaccessible to academic psychology. As academic psychology in India has begun to explore this symbolic and conceptual resource, it has opened up varied possibilities of exciting research propositions. It may be relevant to add in this context that this ancient knowledge has been extended, elaborated, even questioned in the long history. Thinkers and sages of modern times have added and commented on what we know from *Vedas*, *Upanishads*, and different schools of thought. Sri Aurobindo, Ramakrishna, Krishnamurthi, Gandhi are names of a few modern thinkers who have vastly contributed to this ancient wisdom and have been able to present it in a language, which we understand.

Indian psychology is not revivalist, if revivalism means reassertion of the ancient order in the present world. It cannot be an exercise to reconfirm the theories propounded in the ancient texts through scientific methodology, nor does it aim to establish its superiority over other knowledge systems. The challenge before Indian psychology is to carve out the core of this ancient wisdom and develop testable propositions. The study of ancient human science is not merely an academic exercise but it aims to transform self and build a happy, healthy, and harmonious social order. Indian psychology is part of a movement toward contemporizing Indian theories and testing their relevance for enhancing human competencies and well-being. It is the atemporal nature of Indian psychology and its proximity to our essential human nature across ages and geographies that sustain its appeal in the modern times.

Indian Psychology is not a Distinct Branch of Psychology

It may be posited here that Indian psychology does not aspire to be a distinct branch of psychology, like social, personality, and clinical psychologies. Confining Indian psychology to a specific content domain will do injustice to its vast potential and may deprive psychology of its diversity and richness. Indian psychology covers the whole range of human possibilities and, therefore, as a school of thought has relevance for all branches of psychology. It creates new possibilities of looking at the age old human problems of social conflicts and violence, emotional and mental health, human greed and need for individual growth.

Should Indian psychology be bracketed with other cultural psychologies, like Chicano psychology, Chinese psychology, African psychology, Philippine psychology, etc.? It may eventually be put it in an absurd situation in which there are a plethora of psychologies competing with each other for recognition. As discussed earlier, firstly Indian psychology is not conceived as the psychology of Indians, as many other cultural psychologies are. Secondly, Indian psychology spills over in all other branches of psychology and as a holistic field covers the entire psychology tree, be it health, social, mental health, organizational, or any other branch. It is concerned about human growth and welfare to which other psychologies can equally contribute.

Summary and Conclusion

Indian psychology is as old as the Indian civilization but its history as a modern discipline is also as old as that of the Western psychology in India. The new beginning of Indian psychology in the modern times can be traced in the work of Swami Vivekananda, Ramana Maharishi, and Sri Aurobindo in the early part of the last century. Subsequently, the monumental work of

Jadunath Sinha (1958) on Indian psychology, a compilation of psychological concepts and theories in scriptures and other ancient texts, laid its firm foundation. However, it took much longer time for Indian psychology research to build up. It is only in the last decade or so that research in this area has picked up momentum and many important publications have come out. Looking at the plethora of research and publication activities going on at present, it is likely that Indian psychology will have a critical mass sooner than later. As discussed earlier, it is a misnomer that Western psychology is universal and Indian psychology is not. Indian psychology is neither competing nor striving to replace Western psychology as universal science. It only intends to offer an alternative perspective. Whereas Western science has focused on the human problems, Indian psychology primarily looks at the growth aspects, that is, on how human beings can actualize their full potential and can free themselves from their mental conditioning. In this sense Western psychology and Indian psychology can complement each other by bringing into the fold of research the whole range of human possibilities. It is in this respect that Indian psychology claims its legitimate place in a truly global mainstream psychology.

However, despite all possibilities and provocations, Indian psychology is still struggling to make inroads into the academic citadels of Indian universities. There are hardly any places where courses on Indian psychology are being taught, and there is still a good deal of resistance to introduction of Indian psychology into their teaching programmes. Ostensibly, a larger body of Indian psychologists are still wary of the nature and agenda of Indian psychology. There are wide ranges of apprehensions which have stalled the acceptance of a psychology of Indian origin. Some such misconceptions are briefly noted here.

First, Indian theories of mind and consciousness are often held to be subjective and not amenable to scientific testing. Consequently, Indian psychology is considered as not amenable to empirical research using the established scientific methodology. As such, Indian psychology is considered a regressive step, which may reduce the science of psychology to a non-scientific enterprise. Second, a bulk of Indian psychologists are concerned about keeping pace with advancements in empirical research methodology and statistical techniques, which give psychology the status of a highly sophisticated scientific enterprise among all social sciences. Indian psychologists are trained in positivistic methods and are more at ease in employing them. Third, scientific-minded psychologists still consider Indian psychology as part of a religious (worse, revivalist) movement. Many are of the view that the subject matter of Indian psychology is esoteric, mystical, and metaphysical. Therefore, there is an anxiety that including Indian psychology in the academic curriculum would undermine the secular credentials of their scientific pursuits; that such a move may offend the sensibilities of the scientists of other faiths. Fourth, working within the domain of Indian psychology will cut them off from the rest of the world and may label them as being parochial or ethnocentric. This may deprive their research wider transnational recognition and may foreclose the possibilities of international collaboration and support. In fact, many yoga research institutes, like SVYASA, Bangalore are getting international attention on par with the best research institutes in the world. Lastly, there is a practical reason for sticking to Western psychology in academia. There is no tangible incentive to the academic community to change their areas of specialization. It may be more rewarding to do research, for example, in the area of emotional intelligence than, say, detachment. Indian psychologists require sustained efforts to re-educate themselves, which is hard without peer support, reading material, and training programmes. Nandy (1995) has argued that conducting experiments, developing and adapting psychological tests, and mindlessly replicating Western research is what has kept Indian psychologists occupied without any clarity of purpose. These Indian psychologists are often aware that the psychology they are pursuing does not address the real issues of change and development, both at social and individual level. They know that no in-depth analysis of the socio-psychological problems of Indian society will yield from this endeavour. A discontentment is brewing among the psychology fraternity about the state of psychology in India. An urgent need is felt to re-orchestrate the processes of teaching, training, and research in psychology with an open mind and cultural sensibility.

Despite all resistance and setbacks the Indian psychology movement seems to be gathering momentum, if attendance at Indian psychology conferences, workshops, and research publications is taken as an index. There is a good deal of excitement and sense of purpose in the section of psychologists who are pursuing Indian psychology. It can be easily discerned that this newly emerging science of Indian psychology calls for a paradigm shift. We need a serious and sustained debate on nature, characteristics, and implication of this new paradigm. A dominant view is that the Western and the Indian paradigms are irreconcilable and cannot have a meeting ground. Indian concepts and theories are grounded in different notions of the human nature, epistemology, values, and worldview, than the Western ones. However, the range of problems suggests the need for both the paradigms. Whereas the methodology of Western psychology focuses on the study of the 'other' person, Indian psychology (as other Eastern psychologies) focuses on the study of one's 'own-self'. We need both first-person and third-person approaches to bring about the desired changes in human condition. Indian psychology's experiential basis of knowledge generation is common to the theories and practices of many other Eastern philosophies, including Zen, Tao, and Buddhism. The proponents of this position hold that building a more harmonious and conflict-free world order where people are able to actualize their inner potential can be a valid goal. It is hoped that turning toward Indian psychology would help the discipline by expanding the scope of psychological inquiry and offering technologies for self-transformation leading to a better quality of life.

Notes

1. James Mill (1848), in an influential book on the history of British India, throughout referred to Indians as 'rude', 'lazy', 'timid', 'ignorant', and 'prone to flattery'. These claims to Hindu inferiority and British superiority, as reflected in Mill's (1848) work, were largely based on cultural and religious comparisons rather than on racial or physiological differences.
2. In this paper, a distinction is made between spirituality and religion. Whereas religion is an organized, institutionalized activity, spirituality is taken as an individual's quest to know own-self and to carve out their own path to liberation. This has

created confusion in Western psychology in which these two terms are used interchangeably. If we can replace religion with spirituality, a synthesis of science and spirituality is a possibility.

3. It may be interesting to note that the term Buddhist psychology was first used in the translation of Buddhist texts by British Indologists. Goleman expressed it as follows, 'It was news that Buddhism—like many of the world's great spiritual traditions—harboured a theory of mind and its workings' (2004, p. 72).

3

Indian Methods of Knowing

As an ancient science, Indian psychology has some unique features. First, theory and methods are closely intertwined, that is, every theory has its own method of testing its veracity. Nothing is accepted without testing various premises of the theory. Once a theory is formulated it should hold on the crucible of scientific methodology. The method should be objective, systematic, reliable, and yield similar results under controlled conditions. Second, the methodology is consistent with ontology and epistemology of the theory and thus should be part of the paradigm within which the theory is embedded. Theory and methods are in a symbiotic relation, one cannot be understood without understanding the other. Third, subject matter of study in Indian psychology is internal functioning of the mind. The major challenge has been how mind can understand itself? In Western psychology, it is a puzzle how the mind can study itself? When the mind studies itself, all kinds of biases are likely to distort the results. And this dilemma persists till date. In Indian epistemology, a distinction is made between the mind and the consciousness which is considered higher seat of knowing. The consciousness can fathom the structure and functioning of the mind without distorting its reality. The consciousness does reveal the truth which transcends the mind. Fourth, the instruments of inquiry are within the person and it is required to be harnessed for research purpose. Various forms of yoga and meditation developed over thousands of years are used as research tools to examine mental states. The methods of study of the Self are considered different from those of study of the external world. All methods known in the West are considered apt for studying man in the outside world. There are always multiple methods to arrive at the similar results ensuring triangulation. Fifth, the ultimate objective of knowing is to liberate human being from suffering and attain liberation from all human bondages. The goal is to attain state of bliss which is the highest state of being. The methods of Indian psychology lead to human progression to attain human potential and experience ultimate freedom.

Two points need to be kept in mind while discussing research methods in this section. As stated in the beginning of this chapter, Indian psychology has grown around both, the classical and the folk traditions, with a good deal of overlap between the two. However, classical tradition focuses on the study of human consciousness with the goal being transcending to the highest level of spiritual existence. On the other, folk tradition is the psychology of ordinary people living in this mundane world. Methods for these two Indian psychologies overlap but differ in their goals, orientation, and emphasis.

Research in folk psychology, which primarily aims to understand empirical reality, has been using methods of Western psychology. A detailed discussion on these methods can be seen in any standard textbooks of psychology taught in India. These methods comprise both experimental and non-experimental methods of survey, field studies, interviews, case studies, testing, etc. Courses on these scientific methods of research are taught to all students of psychology. These scientific methods are shaped on the assumption of physical sciences that it is possible to find objective reality of human existence. Western psychology has built up on this methodology for almost a century. Cognitive psychology which takes, not objective but perceived reality as the data, also employed the same methods of science. Positivistic (empirical) approach greatly emphasized development and use of tests, scales, and measures in psychological research, including the use of statistical techniques.

In the last three or four decades, a new movement of post-modernism has given rise to a new paradigm of social constructionism. In this paradigm, it is argued that social reality is not like physical reality; it is construed by the researcher for the purpose of theory building and measurement. In this endeavour even the same phenomena—like society, family, emotions, and attitude—are defined in different manner by different researchers. As such, there is no objective reality in psychological research, thus, all interpretations of the data in social sciences are valid in a specific context. This new thinking seriously questions the application of positivistic methods in social sciences and has led to the development of new quantitative methodologies in research.

The Quantitative and Qualitative Divide

In broad terms, all research methods can be classified into two categories—quantitative and qualitative methods, no matter which research paradigm is subscribed to. Research methodology since ancient times, both in East and West, was qualitative in nature, and remained so till modern age when measurement and quantification became the hallmark of science. Commentaries on classical and other texts often followed well laid out rules and practices in every society. Verbal reports used to be the basis of judging people and were important in taking social–political–moral decisions. Students in Socrates' academy and other schools, as well as in the ashrams of sages in India were taught to critic the verbal and written texts but its purpose was to develop a better understanding of the text and integrate it in the body of existing knowledge. Many of these methods are now considered mystical, esoteric, biased, and therefore, unscientific. In the initial phase, scientific psychology in Europe was close to what one would call the qualitative research. In this, verbal report of the 'experiences' by the subject used to be the main body of data. If one closely peruses the research done in Wundtian laboratories, it will be noticed that no clear distinction was made between qualitative and quantitative methods (e.g. Mays and Pope, 1995). Of course, the quantitative and qualitative methods that we employ in research today are, in a way, refinement of many centuries-old practices.

In the last three decades, several new qualitative methods were developed in psychology. Three handbooks, namely, *The Sage Handbook of Qualitative Research* (2005, 3rd edition) and *The Sage Handbook of Qualitative Research in Psychology* (2008), and *The Oxford Handbook of Qualitative Research* (2014) cover the whole range of qualitative methods. The popularity of qualitative methodology is on rise in recent years. Though complementarity of quantitative and qualitative methodologies is emphasized, but it seems for the present, psychology in divided between these two camps with different epistemologies, subject matter, objectives, and implications of the research.

It may be stated here that the term method in quantitative research does not have the same connotation as in qualitative research. Quantitative methods are more structured, with step-by-step procedure laid down, which a researcher can easily learn. In qualitative research, there are no laid-down steps to follow in data analysis. There is much more freedom to researchers in qualitative research to develop their own analysis plan within a broad framework. This built-in flexibility precludes any standardization of analysis procedures, and we can only talk in terms of research methodologies (Dalal and Priya, 2015), broad principles of particular set of methods.

The list of quantitative and qualitative methods can be endlessly large. Here, we are listing some of the prominent research methods from these two categories.

1. *Quantitative methods*: Experimental methods, Qui-experiments, surveys, questionnaires, observation method, test construction and testing, field studies, etc.
2. *Qualitative methods*: Qualitative methods are of two types:
   (a) *Positivistic*: Content analysis, ethnography, projective tests, case studies, and archival research.
   (b) *Constructionist*: Grounded theory, narrative research, focus group discussion, ethno-methodology, discourse analysis, phenomenological research, conversational analysis, visual–textual analysis, etc.

Coming to the methods of Indian psychology of consciousness, the methodology pitches at a different level, where the subject matter of study is inside the person. Indian ontology of what constitutes a person is radically different from that of the

Western. The supremacy of consciousness in Indian systems requires major change in the methodology of research. Methodologies in the guise of yoga and meditation have evolved for ages, to develop awareness of this consciousness and through the direct, unmediated knowledge of reality. While engaging in this discussion, it may be reiterated that Western scientific knowledge is out there, whereas it is a matter of personal awareness in Indian thought systems. Also Western methods of knowledge are informative, whereas Indian methods are transformative in nature. The main purpose of these methods of yoga and meditation is to bring change in own self, as one better understands the reality of one's existence. These methods vary from one school to another; sometimes even within the school. For example, the methods of *tantra* vary in different regions and sects. Indeed there are mindboggling varieties of methodologies in Indian psychology which claim their efficiency in bringing about the desired change. In the last 800 years of the dark age of Indian psychology, many spurious methods have cropped up which needed to be weeded out through systematic examination and develop new one. In the last century, many sages and yoga practitioners have done many innovations in the techniques of yoga and meditation, which need to be systematically documented.

A Three-Fold Classification

Taking the whole gamut of research methodologies for Indian psychology, a different way of classifying research methods is followed here. This scheme of classifying research methods is in terms of researcher–participant dichotomy. The question is on whom the research is conducted and by whom? Following the natural science model of research, psychological research is mostly conducted on the 'other person' under controlled conditions. It is only in last two or three decades that psychologists have paid attention to other modes of conducting research. Taking together, the positivistic, constructionist, and yoga (to be discussed in the later section) paradigms of research can be examined in terms of *who* is the researcher. A three-fold classification of research methodologies is suggested along this line. These three folds are third-person, second-person and first-person research methodologies. This broader classification scheme should be appropriate to cover all possible methodologies which can be used to study the person. These three folds refer to the following: (a) the researcher and respondent are separate, (b) both are co-researchers, and (c) research on own-self. Depending on the mode of participation of the researcher in the psychological research, purpose and procedure of research will change. Research at these three levels differs in its orientation, purpose, process and interpretation of results.

Third-Person Methodologies

Psychology is primarily the study of other's behaviour and attitudes. The research is conducted on people selected as research participants. Proper sampling procedure is used to identify the target groups and then volunteers are selected to participate in the research from these groups. Data collected on those samples of participants, is then processed and analysed by the researcher. In most of the psychological research this distinction between the researcher and the subject (respondent) is maintained with role clarity and assigned responsibilities. Of course, such research can be conducted on a single respondent.

Such third-person methodologies, as taken from the natural sciences, are also quite widespread in psychology. For instance, two of the main criteria of goodness in constructing psychological tests are *objectivity* (it should not matter who conducts the test, who evaluates the test results), and *reliability* (e.g. if the test is administered again, the similar results should be obtained). Also, all possible influences of the experimenter in psychological research are usually regarded as 'nuisance variables' and should be strictly controlled. This makes sense for examining a wide variety of psychological hypotheses, and often, the influence of extraneous variables (e.g. demographic background the experimenter and the participants) are systematically controlled.

Most of the research methods employed in academic or mainstream psychology belong to this category. It includes both quantitative and qualitative methods, where it is the person (respondent) other than the researcher who is the source of data.

Second-Person Methodologies

Second-person methodologies are participatory in nature; in this the distinction of researcher and respondent is blurred. Both work together as co-researchers in the research process to arrive at some collective solutions emanating from shared experiences. It is a dynamic process of sense-making in which participants interact in the spirit of a collaborative enterprise, elicit data, even using experimental method, to answer the research questions. In second-person research, critical aspect is to build intersubjective reality through collaborative activity, so as to arrive at collective solutions. Such groups could be dyads, triads, or bigger groups which interact in a research according to some plan. For example, some practitioners of yoga may like to test efficacy of a new method of meditation. They may discuss and agree upon a procedure to test it. They may meditate separately and then come to share their experience to test its efficacy and improvise it. People may share a common background, common interest, but still some amount of groundwork (or familiarity) is often a prerequisite to apply second-person methods.

Such participatory methods often aim to engage all stakeholders to collectively search for the solution of practical problems. As such, no distinction is made between researchers and subjects as both work together to study the problem. The focus is primarily on the experiential knowledge for action and growth. The process of research is demystified in which all seekers have equal stake. The newly developing participatory methods (Priya, 2010) and the method of cooperative inquiry (Heron, 1996), in which participants take multiple roles as researchers and as subjects, can be effectively used to study whole range of cultural issues in health research. Such methods are still at the developmental stage.

Second-person approaches to study consciousness are proposed by Depraz (1999) and many others. All these methods need to fulfil two conditions:

1. Providing a clear *procedure* for accessing some phenomenal domain.
2. Providing clear means for an *expression and validation* of the findings by a community of observers who have familiarity with procedures as in (1).

These two conditions are relevant for other second-person methods as well. Validation of such studies can either be done by having several 'second persons' interact with the same participant, having one 'second person' interact with several participants, or a combination of the two. Many of such methods have been used in anthropological and sociological research, which in recent times, are borrowed and modified to be appropriate for psychological research.

First-Person Methodologies

These are pertaining to the methods employed to conduct experiments on own-self. In these studies, research is conducted to understand own physiological, psychological, paranormal, and other kind of inner experiences. Ebbinghaus was the first psychologist who conducted memory experiments on himself.

The forerunner of first-person methodologies was the introspection method. Introspection was introduced by Wilhelm Wundt in his Leipzig laboratories, where one attends carefully to one's own sensation and reports them as objectively as possible. The subjects were required to describe the felt sensation and not the stimulus that provokes it.

In India, yoga and meditation have been used for the exploration of inner experiences as first-person methodology. As methods of research, yoga and meditation have been used for centuries to test, experiment, and arrive at an experiential validation of the higher mental states. Various systems of yoga in India have been developed by systematic, rigorous, and efficient use of such first-person methodologies. In the present times, such methods may be helpful in addressing deeper questions regarding illness, health, and well-being. A major challenge of the first-person methodologies is expression and validation of self-reported experiences. To make the first-person approach a rigorous research means that its results are shared by others, and are supported by similar experiments by others on themselves.

Sri Aurobindo has made a significant contribution to first-person methodology discourse by developing intuition as a potent method of knowing. This method, according to Sri Aurobindo, is a trans-sensory method of knowing. In the ordinary sense we can call it knowledge through intuition and other extra-sensory means. This is a new way of knowing in which senses are not involved. Sri Aurobindo called it knowledge by identity, where we understand by being one with the object of knowing. Sri Aurobindo showed how, through yogic methods, intuition can become a permanent state of one's being, a direct source of knowledge about the world and reality.

Yoga as a first-person methodology can be of help in bridging the gap between first- and third-person methodologies. Yoga methods can be of help in studying subjective experiences as objective reality, which can be corroborated by an independent observer. In the studies of pain and suffering, empathic observer are found to corroborate the first-person experience. Buddhist techniques of exploration of human suffering, which have been tested and refined over twenty-five centuries by many generations of practitioners, provide us with invaluable leads to be pursued further. Such experiments can be conducted only when a researcher is also a practitioner of yoga to attain higher goals of life.

However, despite some reservations as mentioned earlier, it is evident that mainstream science can greatly benefit from the practical knowledge of first- and second-person methods that have accumulated outside its traditional remit. The depth and range of the anecdotal evidence provided by many of the authors in this volume offers a number of fascinating starting points for more rigorous scientific studies. One of the challenges before health psychology is that of the first- and second-person verification of the third-person research. This aspect of first-person methodology needs further elaboration in cases of specific techniques. At present, we know very little about first-person methodology and much work is needed to elaborate and develop such techniques in future.

Indian Methods of Knowing

In the Indian tradition, a distinction is made between *parā vidyā* (knowledge of the self) and *aparā vidyā* (empirical knowledge) (Paranjpe, 1984). *Aparā vidyā* constitutes of the knowledge of the social–physical world we live in and includes science and technology. This knowledge is also relevant to the problems and challenges of the world we live in. The methods of knowing in the empirical world (*pramāṇa*) are diverse and they treat mind (*mānas* or *antaḥkaranā*) as one sensory channel, which allows the understanding of pleasure and pain. *Para vidya* is the knowledge of one's higher existence, beyond the empirical world. It is the knowledge of one's higher consciousness; knowledge of that which is permanent and imperishable. Here, not only the very 'object' of knowledge is very different, but the approach and methodologies are also different. In this case, the knower is striving to know about own-self.

It is clear that academic (Western) psychology has only focussed on surface reality or outer appearance. The deeper reality has escaped the attention of psychologists. Even in the study of yoga and meditation, the focus was only on physiological outcomes and on those psychological aspects which could be easily measured. Also, overemphasis on objectivity led to research outcomes which were trivial and dubious, contradictory, and at the best 'obvious'. It avoided venturing into non-physical reality, mystical experiences, and paranormal phenomena, which are of interest in Indian psychology. Indian psychology is spiritual and transcendental in its orientation in which the unity of spirit and matter—the union of *puruṣha* and *prakṛti*—comprises overall human existence, who is the supreme consciousness in each one of us, and is considered to be the real knower. Waking or sensory consciousness is taken as only one kind of consciousness in Indian scriptures. In contemporary psychology, it is taken as a given reality, a universal standard against which all psychological theories and knowledge should be validated.

Different schools of thought had subscribed to different kind of methodologies. The *Carvaka* school regards perception alone; the Buddhists regard perception and inference; the *Sankhya* and the *Yoga* schools regard perception, inference, and testimony; the *Mimamsa* and the *Advaita Vedantic* schools regard perception, inference, comparison, testimony, presumption, and non-apprehension—as the sources of valid knowledge. This list can be still longer if we also include the methods listed in other texts.

Brief descriptions of these seven methods are given in Table 3.1.

It may be mentioned here that whereas in the Western science the emphasis is on empiricism, and is considered to be the best method of knowing, in Indian tradition intuition is the most preferred and reliable method. Intuitive knowledge is the direct knowledge without any median, and therefore uncontaminated by the sensory environment. The *Nyaya* school has discussed these Indian methods of inquiry at great length.

Table 3.1

Methods of Knowing

	Method	Description
1.	*Pratyakṣa* (empirical, perception, observation)	Objective knowledge of some object through sense organs—perception of both external and internal (bodily) objects and states through the mediation of mind
2.	*Anumāna* (Inference)	Relation between what is perceived and what is deduced—knowledge derived from some other knowledge —through reasoning—both inductive and deductive reasoning
3.	*Upamāna* (Comparison)	Similarity, analogy, or contrast—mind draws parallels
4.	*Arthāpatti* (Postulation)	Developing premises—bridging the gap in our knowledge through assumptions and suppositions
5.	*Śabda pramāṇa* (Verbal testimony)	Acceptance of the testimony of an authority (scriptures, specialist, expert and wise persons who have attained knowledge). Accumulated knowledge through centuries of experience and experimentation —rishis, yogis, gurus, and others
6.	*Anupalabdhi* (Non-cognition)	Knowledge of non-existence
7.	Intuition	Trans-sensory knowledge, non-mediated direct knowledge

Yoga and Meditation as Research Methods: An Indian Paradigm

India has a centuries-old tradition of yoga and meditation with many different systems of practices. Buddhism, Jainism, Shaiva, and other schools of thought have contributed to yoga and meditational practices. Yoga is primarily considered to be a spiritual practice of attaining enlightenment and liberation (Patanjali). Yoga and meditation, in the long history, have been used for improving mental and physical health, by controlling mental and bodily processes. They have been used for dealing with health problems as well. Yoga and meditational techniques are now used all over the world for therapeutic purposes.

Yoga and meditation have also been used for exploration of inner experiences, as first-person methodology. As methods of research, yoga and meditation have been used for centuries to test, experiment, and arrive at an experiential validation of the higher mental states. The various systems of yoga in India have developed rigorous and effective methods of enquiry in the domains of consciousness studies and psychology that may help us find answers to our deepest questions regarding values, truth, love, meaning, and beauty. They can offer to modern science not only a wealth of philosophical and psychological theories, but also a rich store of practical techniques to raise our individual and collective consciousness. Consciousness in the Indian context refers to the awareness one has of one's own existence (being) and its connectedness with the Supreme Being.

The purpose of yoga is to keep refining the inner instrument perceiving and knowing, so that one can have a clearer understanding of inner processes. This instrument of observing is higher consciousness which is independent of waking or sensory consciousness. Sensory consciousness or mind primarily works through sensory inputs and our accumulated memory which is an accumulation of our past experiences and their interpretations, by our upbringing, background, religion, attitudes, and all host of other considerations. Any observation and knowledge emanating from this sensory mind is bound to be biased and unreliable. It is the higher consciousness, which is independent of sensory mind, that is presumed to be neutral, and can, as a witness, observe mental processes and experiences. Yoga techniques are meant to clean this instrument so that, like a mirror, higher consciousness only reflects the reality.

Sri Aurobindo has made a significant contribution to methodology discourse by developing intuition as a potent method of knowing. According to Sri Aurobindo, the higher consciousness of a person can grasp the essence of matter in a way which has till date escaped the physicists, who for the most part acknowledge that they have no idea what matter or energy is in itself (Collected Works of Sri Aurobindo, Volume 17).

This method, according to Sri Aurobindo, is a trans-sensory method of knowing. In the ordinary sense, we can call it knowledge through intuition and other extra-sensory means. This is a new way of knowing in which senses are not involved. Sri Aurobindo called it knowledge by identity, where we understand by being one with the object of knowing. Sri Aurobindo showed how, through yoga, intuition can become a permanent state of one's being, a direct source of knowledge about the world and reality.

While concluding this discussion on Indian methods of knowing it has to be kept in minds that, though these methods have been practiced for centuries to investigate consciousness, paranormal phenomena, and spiritual experiences, their access is limited to serious seekers only. They are part of an established spiritual tradition whose main objective is self-growth and development. A major challenge is to bring these methods within the ambit of scientific psychology by removing ideological overtones. For this, it is necessary that these Indian methods are critically examined within contemporary discourse on the scientific epistemology of self-inquiry.

Yoga as a first-person methodology can be of help in bridging the gap between first- and third-person methodologies. Yoga methods can be of help in studying subjective experiences as objective reality, which can be corroborated by an independent observer. In the studies of pain and suffering, empathic observers are found to corroborate the first-person experience. Buddhist techniques of exploration of human suffering, which have been tested and refined over twenty-five centuries by many generations of practitioners, provide us with invaluable leads to pursue. But mastering meditation techniques requires intensive training for several years which is impracticable for most of the health scientists. Nevertheless, methods of yoga gives scientists some hope that proper methodologies can be developed for collecting the data (both first and third person), express them in suitable language and find connecting principles. We need to work on a 'fundamental theory of consciousness', that is, to unravel universal laws of the interconnected world. One problem is that yoga methodology is integral to India's spiritual tradition and how far such methodology can be reconciled with rationale theories of the West?

4

A Science in Search of Its Identity

Twentieth Century Psychology in India

Academic psychology in India has continued to be an alien discipline throughout this century. Western concepts and theories have provided the basis on which Indian research has been built. Concerns have been voiced from time to time to align psychology with contemporary social reality, so as to meet the challenges of rapid socio-economic changes. Looking back, one does not get the impression that psychology in India has chartered a long distance in this direction despite a vast volume of research output. Though there are many exceptions, psychology in India has largely remained a sterile academic pursuit. Indian psychologists are yet to establish that they have adequate motivation, conceptual tools, and expertise to grapple with the real issues in national development. The absence of psychologists in various national programmes gives rise to serious concern about its relevance and redemption. What kind of psychology we aspire to have in the twenty-first century is contingent on a better understanding of the present state-of-the-art. This article aims at examining the status of psychology in India as a scientific discipline of the twentieth century, identifying the factors responsible for its failure to address the burning social issues in a significant way.

Earlier version of this chapter was published as 'Dalal, A.K. (1996). A science in search of its identity: Twentieth century psychology in India. *Indian Psychological Abstracts and Reviews*, 3, 201–44'.

Three sets of arguments are put forward to explain this failure of psychology in India. One is the lack of a supportive intellectual climate. In a country, where a vast population lives under subhuman poverty conditions and decisions about social development programmes are politically motivated, any scholarly pursuit is considered peripheral. The academic institutions plagued by increasing student unrest, political manipulations, and lack of funds have gradually become non-performers. There is no premium on excellence in teaching and research. Adair et al. (1995) conducted a study of psychologists through mailed questionnaire and revealed three major impediments to research productivity which are as follows: (i) lack of a supportive intellectual climate, (ii) poor professional support, and (iii) inadequate research funding. Ostensibly, lack of an academic culture and non-supportive political environment were found to be greatly responsible for the prevailing state of affairs. It does explain the overall decline of the academic standards in the country. It, however, throws no light on 'why psychology in India is lagging behind other sister disciplines, such as sociology and economics?' It brings forth the second line of argument that there are some inherent limitations of psychology as a scientific discipline. Its excessive conformity to empirical methodologies and confinement to only micro-level problems has restricted the scope of its psychosocial inquiry. The methodological progress is woefully inadequate to address more applied macro-level problems. The restricted boundaries of the discipline obviate the need to work in applied settings, or to work with governmental or non-governmental agencies. The third set of arguments focuses on the personal and professional background of Indian psychologists in the first half of this century who were products of colonial domination of Indian society, greatly influenced by Western scholarly traditions. The first-generation psychologists after India's Independence were predominantly converts from philosophy background. This, coupled with their elitist urban background, few job openings, and self-serving research orientation gave Indian psychologists an identity distinct from those who belonged to other sister disciplines. This article examines the progress of psychology in India against the backdrop of these arguments. It endeavours to explore the possibilities of psychology becoming a more vibrant science, accepting the challenges of the rapidly changing Indian society.

This exercise is particularly relevant in the light of the fact that psychology as an academic discipline is completing 80 years of existence and is preparing to enter into the twenty-first century. The first psychology department with master's and doctoral programmes was established in 1916 at the Calcutta University. Two more departments were established at Mysore and Patna Universities before Independence in 1947. At present, there are 67 universities' departments offering advanced courses in various fields of psychology. India has the largest number of psychologists outside the Western bloc countries and is considered a 'publication giant' among all developing countries (Gilgin and Gilgin, 1987). This rapid expansion of the discipline has raised many hopes and expectations about its possible contribution to the success of national programmes of socio-economic development. There is a growing realization that solution to the pressing problems of poverty, overpopulation, illiteracy, urban decay, and disease control depends not just on sound economic planning, but also on bringing desirable changes in the attitudes and beliefs of the people, and their motivations for collective action. This calls for a realistic appraisal of the impediments which psychology in India is currently experiencing.

In recent years many good publications have appeared to enable a critical evaluation of the development of psychology in India. Some of these writings (Dalal, 1990; Ganguli, 1971; Misra and Gergen, 1993; Nandy, 1974; D. Sinha, 1986, 1994; J.B.P. Sinha, 1993) have critically evaluated the progress of psychology since its inception in the twentieth century. The three surveys of research in psychology (Mitra, 1972; Pandey, 1981; Pareek, 1980) cover important research contributions. Pareek and Rao (1974a), Pestonjee (1986), and the NCERT (1981) have compiled most of the psychological measures developed in India. Reports prepared by the University Grants Commission (UGC, 1968, 1982) deal with teaching and research programmes in universities. Some empirical studies (Adair, 1990; Pareek, Dixit, and Saruparjya, 1979; Singh and Dalal, 1988) have examined the professional status of the discipline of psychology. These publications form the basis of this article.

In brief, this article traces the genesis of scientific psychology in India in the beginning of this century. It examines the constraints and creative pursuits of Indian psychologists in seeking a disciplinary identity. It reviews the state of research, teaching, and professional bodies of the discipline of psychology. Lastly, some conjectures are made about the possible directions in which psychology is likely to tread in the coming century.

Indian scriptures dating back thousands of years extensively dealt with the analysis of states and contents of mental activities. The important feature of this early exposition is that it is largely experiential and is a culmination of centuries-old tradition of self-verification. In the ancient Indian scriptures, there were no rigid distinctions between religion, philosophy, and psychology. The overriding consideration was to help individuals in their pursuit of self-realization and liberation from the miseries of life. In this worldview, the sources of all suffering was presumed to be within the person, and thus the emphasis was on exploring the 'world within', to alleviate the suffering. The goal was to seek enduring harmony of spirit, mind, and body for lasting happiness. The yoga system evolved very sophisticated mind control techniques in this pursuit. In contemporary literature this broad field of inquiry is referred to as Indian psychology.

These rich traditions, however, had little bearing on academic psychology implanted in India as a Western science during the British rule. Scientific psychology with laboratory work was a novel approach, not having any parallel in traditional Indian psychology. Psychology was first introduced as a subject in the Philosophy Department at Calcutta University. Sir Brojendra Nath Seal, who was the then King George V Professor of Mental and Moral Philosophy at the Calcutta University drafted the first syllabus for experimental psychology and established a laboratory in 1905. Eleven years later, this laboratory was upgraded as the first psychology department, named the Department of Experimental psychology. Narendra Nath Sengupta, who chaired this department, had received his education at Harvard University with Hugo Munsterberg, a student of Wilhelm Wundt. Laboratory research at Calcutta in the areas of depth perception, psychophysics, and attention inspired early work at other centres. Recognizing the scientific nature of research, psychology was included as a separate section in the Indian Science Congress in 1923.

Thus, psychology in India at an early stage acquired the status of a science along with physical and biological sciences, something which Western psychology could achieve only after a long struggle. The Indian Psychological Association was founded in 1924 and the *Indian Journal of Psychology,* the first psychology journal in India, appeared in the following year.

Before these experimental traditions could be consolidated, Sengupta left Calcutta. He was succeeded by Girindra Shekhar Bose. Being a psychiatrist who was in close contact with Sigmund Freud, Bose showed much enthusiasm to promote psychoanalysis. In 1922, he founded the Indian Psychoanalytic Society, which was affiliated with the International Psychoanalytic Society in 1924. Bose obtained his doctoral degree from Calcutta on the 'concept of repression', the first doctorate from any Indian university in psychology. He also established Lumbini Park Mental Hospital in Calcutta in 1940, and in 1947 launched a journal *Samiksha.* The department started an Applied psychology Wing in 1938, when Jung, Meyers, and Spearman were invited to the Silver Jubilee Session of the Indian Science Congress.

Prior to India's Independence, other departments were established at Mysore and Patna Universities. M.V. Gopalswami, who headed the department at Mysore, was trained at London University with Spearman in mental testing tradition. He developed Indian adaptations of Western intelligence tests and applied psychological principles in the field of education. Gopalswami was first to set up an animal laboratory in India. The department at Patna began in 1946, along with the Institute of Psychological Research and Services headed by H.P. Maiti. Vocational guidance and counselling was provided to a large number of students as well as to the general public. Since Maiti had been trained by Girindra Shekhar Bose, his orientation was psychoanalytic and clinical. In a short time, Patna emerged as a major centre for teaching, research, and counselling services.

Research during this period was mainly in the areas of sensation, perception, psychophysics, and reaction time (Banerjee, 1932; Pal, 1936), which were influenced by the work of Wundt and Titchner. Fascination for laboratory work and value-free research based on the natural science model sustained the interest of Indian psychologists in these areas. Western research in these areas could easily be replicated without due consideration to cultural variables. In the area of social psychology, early work focussed on replicating Allport's experiments on social facilitation on Indian samples (Sengupta and Sinha, 1926). An important work of this period was the rumour study by Prasad (1935). Prasad analysed the rumours during a major earthquake in North India. He found that most rumours were anxiety-inducing, thereby justifying the fear experienced by earthquake victims. D. Sinha (1952) also conducted a rumour study along similar lines. Festinger acknowledged that this work inspired his formulation of cognitive dissonance theory (Cohen and Cohen, 1977).

Two Worlds of Indian Psychologists

The development of social sciences and psychology in particular, is based on the principles of capitalism, individualism, and secularism all of which were byproducts of the industrial revolution in Europe. The ideas, concepts, and theories in Western psychology have their genesis in the social upheavals in Europe in nineteenth century following the metamorphosis of society from an agrarian to an industrial one. The discipline evolved to comprehend the complex social realities and the problems of industrialization. With the imperial expansion of modern capitalism, the influence of Western knowledge base on colonized societies was inevitable. The popularity of English-medium education made writings of Western thinkers accessible to Indian scholars. A large body of this knowledge was alien, even in contradiction with that which was prevalent in colonized traditional societies. The contradictions were even more glaring in colonies like India, which had a strong sense of cultural identity and a rich heritage of scholarly work.

In the West, psychology had already moved away from theology and philosophy, and had developed its own methods of inquiry based on the natural science models. Indian psychologists, saw, in applying Western psychology, an opportunity of developing secular identity distinct from religious and philosophy, which was not possible within the indigenous intellectual tradition, integrating spiritually, philosophy, and psychology. Moreover, due to the neglect of many centuries, Indian psychology was not equipped to examine the contemporary world and did not have the contemporary tools to explain existing social and moral decay of Indian society. There were no new concepts, theories, and methods in Indian psychology applicable to the changing individual and society. Aligning with Western positivism gave Indian psychologists fresh opportunities to make a new beginning. The emerging positive science discipline of psychology gave rise to expectations of generating radically different expectations of prolonging colonial rule. There are exciting possibilities of making important discoveries about Indian people and society. Also, one could hope that the explanations of positive science will provide much-needed respectability to Indian cultural practices and rituals. At a personal level, it imparted a new respectability to the upwardly mobile psychology professionals who mostly belong to upper class Western educated elite. As Nandy (1995) has stated in the context of Girindra Shekhar Bose, there was an awareness that sectoral and one dimensional approach of academic psychology could neither yield in-depth analysis of socio-psychological problems of Indian society, nor could it establish durable links with Indian traditions and belief systems.

Nandy (1995) has further stated, 'As a result of this unusual encounter between an ancient civilization and own distinct culture of science and an exogenous science with its distinctive culture fractured the self-definition not only of Bose but of many others involved in the similar enterprise' (p. 83). Caught between two worlds, Indian psychologists always had a problem of balancing a number of polarities—metaphysical versus empirical, clinical versus empirical, and intuitive versus objective. The Indian mind, even if trained to be a scientist, often finds it difficult to ruthlessly pursue the objective reality which comes naturally to a Westerner. Thus for an Indian, conflicting elements are resolved into a suspension rather than a solution. 'The aesthetic satisfaction of a Hindu myth resides in full savouring of both the extremes rather than seeking a synthesis' (Kakar, 1982a, p. 11). Indian psychologists compartmentalized their work in Western psychological tradition from scholarly and personally satisfying creative pursuits. They simultaneously lived in two different worlds without any significant overlap.

Indian psychologists before Independence lived in two different worlds that can be illustrated with some examples.

Brojendra Nath Seal, who established the first psychology laboratory in the country to promote experimental psychology, was a great historian of ancient Indian science and was an inspiration for Jadunath Sinha to bring out a seminal work on Indian psychology. N.N. Sengupta, trained as an experimental psychologist had a large number of non-empirical papers in scientific journals. His papers covered a wide spectrum of publications from psychology of mysticism to psychology of Western dance. Sengupta, however, did not remain in Kolkata for long and took up an administrative post in Lucknow University. It was here that he came in contact with an eminent sociologist, Radhakamal Mukerjee and co-authored a book with him on social psychology in 1928. The orientation of this book was sociological than psychological. Girindra Shekhar Bose, along with his important work in the area of psychoanalysis, serialized a commentary on the *Bhagavad Gita* in the prestigious Bengali magazine, *Pravasi*, without reference to psychoanalytic concepts (Nandy, 1995). Bose also wrote a 300-page long book in Bengali, entitled *Purana Pravesha*, a commentary on Indian sacred texts and epics. Gopalswami, who was at Mysore came from an affluent background and maintained an interest in two diverse fields—intelligence testing and animal laboratory work. He had his own private radio station and was equally involved in cultural activities.

These illustrations are cited to give some clues about how Indian psychologists managed to live simultaneously in two worlds with little overlap. It is no surprise that Indian psychologists remained apolitical all along eventful history. There is no reflection in their work of the predominant social and political movements, even that of the freedom movement. Indian psychologists remained on the periphery of society as far as their professional activities were concerned. Their research lacked continuity, commitment, and conviction. The situation changed only marginally after Independence.

One reason why Indian psychologists could live in two parallel worlds, was probably because the colonial rulers did not see much utility of psychology in consolidating their empire. This, for example, was not true in the case of sociology and social anthropology, which had much to contribute to the smooth functioning of colonial administration in India (Dhanagare,

1985). The colonial rulers were completely unfamiliar with the Indian culture and society when they first arrived. The unique systems of caste, religion, tribal and rural communities, rituals, beliefs, and traditions were baffling to an Englishman. It had no parallel in the experiences of Western societies. Thus, in the absence of an adequate understanding of Indian social realities, the colonial administrators faced many problems. There was an urgency and support for research on these topics. Neither Indian psychology nor Western psychological research held any such promise and were largely ignored. It is understandable that the British did not promote psychology in India the same way as they did sociology and social anthropology.

In fact, Indian culture with its liberal and multiple traditions did not offer resistance to this newly emerging science. In the West, Descartesan psychology had to face stiff opposition from theology for a long time. Psychoanalysis had a very controversial entry in Western society; many of Freud's works were initially banned in European countries. In India, on the other hand, his work was accepted without any resistance. The three main streams of academic psychology in India—experimental psychology, psychoanalysis, and intelligence testing—were viewed as culture-free, justifying uncritical borrowing from the West.

The fact that psychologists in India lived in two worlds did not change much after Independence, it rather became more pronounced. In most universities, psychology departments were established by splitting philosophy departments. As a result, the bulk of the philosophy faculty moved to the newly formed psychology departments; many who opted for psychology obviously perceived attractive career opportunities in the newly carved out departments. This movement from philosophy to psychology was so pervasive that by the end of 1960s a majority of chairmen of psychology departments were trained in philosophy. Normally, it was expected that they would bring a strong philosophical knowledge base to psychology, making it richer in terms of indigenous concepts and theories. But this did not happen. In their enthusiasm to establish a new identity for themselves as scientists, the new psychology faculty completely dissociated themselves from their parent discipline. They were more fascinated by the idea of value-free and culturally neutral experimental work. The areas that attracted their attention were memory, psychophysics, perception, learning, pattern recognition, etc., which could be studied without bringing in the cultural context. These faculty from philosophy had little training in research methodology. Their major quest, therefore, was to acquire methodological sophistication and mastery over statistical techniques. In the process they became ardent adherents of Western research methods. Thus, despite their firm moorings in ancient Indian psychology, psychology in India did not reap the fruits of this unique advantage. Indian psychologists continued to coexist in two different worlds. As professionals they were engaged in scientific research based on Western models but to satisfy their creative urges they would engage in other activities. This Indian experience was not atypical in this respect. In Pakistan (Ansari, 1990) and Bangladesh (Begum, 1990) also it was the same story, as in many other former colonies.

Response to the Call of Relevance

Following India's Independence in 1947, there was some change in the content and concerns of psychological research. The national government recognized the importance of social science teaching and research in attaining the objective of national reconstruction and social development. There were great hopes and expectations about the role which social sciences could play in this endeavour. Psychologists began to realize that they had a responsibility to change their approach to research in socially relevant direction.

For instance, psychologists responded to the human tragedy of the partition of India. As an aftermath, thousands were killed in Hindu–Muslim riots, and there was a mass exodus of refugee from across the border. Many psychological studies of that period evidenced this concern, such as problem of rehabilitation of human society (Naidu, 1947), impact of the variability to population change (Geddes, 1947), Hindu–Muslim tension (Dosajh, 1953), and psychological conditions of peace (Loomba, 1946). Realizing the urgent need of research in this area, the Ministry of Education procured the services of Gardner Murphy through UNESCO in 1950 to develop a research programme to investigate the causes of communal violence. Many Indian psychologists collaborated on this project which culminated in the publication of a books *In the Minds of Men* (Murphy, 1953). Many

Indian psychologists continued to work in this area in later years, for example, research on communal tension in India (Ram, 1955), and the study of intercaste tension in villages (Singh, 1969). More recently, Kakar (1996) has proposed a psychoanalytic explanation of the rise of communal tension in the wake of Ram Janmabhumi–Babari Masjid dispute.

Another area which emerged during this period but did not sustain in later decades is counselling and guidance. The guidance bureau at Patna inspired the establishment of similar bureaus in other states. The UP Psychological Bureau was among the first one to be established in 1947. This bureau under the leadership of Sohan Lal and later under C.M. Bhatia and B.N. Malhotra adopted many intelligence and aptitude tests in Hindi and provided counselling services to the public. The Bihar Psychological Bureau under the guidance of Mohsin worked under similar lines. In Mumbai the Parsi Panchayat Vocational Guidance Bureau provided services to students, as well as to referred cases. The Bureau also published the *Journal of Vocational and Educational Guidance.* This journal played an important role in promoting the guidance movement in the country. However, the social and political conditions were just not conducive for expansion of this movement and not enough research was built up to sustain the movement. Consequently, the movement lost its momentum (Sinha, 1986). The first CSSR surveys of research in psychology are testimony to the fact that this area did not yield much research in later years. Realizing the urgent need of research in this area, a new development after Independence was the growth of psychology outside the university system. The Ahmedabad Textile Industries Research Association (ATIRA) was established in 1950, where Kamla Chowdhury conducted large scale surveys to study motivational problems in textile industries. Erikson and McClelland were frequent visitors to this Institute. In the clinical field, advanced training programmes were introduced at the All India Institute of Mental Health (now known as the National Institute of Mental Health and Neuro-Sciences) in 1955, followed by the Hospital for Mental Diseases in Ranchi in 1962. The Indian Armed Forces also evinced an interest in using psychological tests for personnel selection. For this, the Psychological Research Wing of the Defence Science Organisation was set up in 1949. The aim of this wing was not only to help in the selection of army personnel, but also to conduct research on range of defence related problems, such as motivation and morale of the armed forces, leadership, mental health, stress, rehabilitation of disabled war veterans, and development of psychological tests. Later, this wing was elevated as the Defence Institute of Psychological Research which employs a large number of psychologists.

These efforts and opportunities reveal the contribution which psychology could make in different domains of national life. Psychology as a discipline was somehow not equipped to seize these initiatives. The poor training and replicative nature of research did not prepare psychologists to confront real life problems. However, few psychologists participated in developmental programmes, but on the whole the discipline remained on the periphery.

It was the time when other social scientists, such as sociologists and economists had already started making their presence felt. For psychologists, it was a case of one more missed opportunity.

Rapid but Unplanned Expansion

In the 1950s and 1960s the growth of psychology in Indian universities was phenomenal. The UGC was constituted in 1956 and it provided funds to various universities to establish psychology departments. As a result, by the end of the 1950s there were 15 universities offering programmes in psychology. The number of departments increased to 32 by the end of 1960s.

The rapid expansion of psychology, though impressive, was quite unplanned. In the absence of any definite educational policy of the government, these departments were created as part of the general expansion of higher education; many times due to non-academic considerations. No serious thinking proceeded in establishing these departments in terms of their need-based specialization. Nevertheless, in the course of their growth many departments developed a distinct identity (Pandey, 1969). For example, several departments became known for their research work in the areas of rural and social psychology (Allahabad), test construction (Mysore), industrial psychology (Osmania), measurement and guidance (Patna), and verbal learning (Poona). Most departments developed around one dominant scholar, usually the person heading the department. His interest and training were decisive factors in the specialization of that department. Psychology during those days (this is more or less true even today) developed around personalities, and when those scholars departed, many centres either collapsed or the area of specialization changed.

In the late 1960s, concerned about the declining standards of university departments and to facilitate research programmes, the UGC launched a new scheme of Centres for Advanced Studies and Centres for Special Assistance. Under these schemes two psychology departments (at Utkal and Allahabad Universities) were elevated to the status of Centre of Advanced Studies in Psychology. The idea was to develop some departments as research centres at par with the best in the world with the help of liberal government support. Departments at Delhi, Gorakhpur, and Tirupati were also elevated to the status of Centre of Special Assistance, a penultimate stage to receiving the Advanced Centre status. These departments were expected to provide leadership in the areas of research, teaching and professional activities.

Though the practice of going abroad for higher education was an old one, a significant development after Independence was the introduction of a number of educational exchange programmes. The most sought after were the fellowships of Commonwealth, Fulbright, and Ford Foundation. A number of bilateral academic exchange programmes were commissioned by the UGC and the Ministry of Education, Government of India. Under these schemes a large number of Indian scholars went to Britain, Canada, and the United States for doctoral and postdoctoral training in the 1960s and 1970s. Upon their return, these scholars were appointed to academic posts; they not only had better training in research techniques but also brought along contemporary research ideas, and continued academic collaboration with their seminal professors abroad. This brought about qualitative changes in teaching and research. Under these exchange programmes many Western scholars also visited Indian universities. Psychology in India for another two decades was dominated by scholars trained abroad. Equipped with recently acquired expertise in Western theories and methods, they evinced a keen interest in applying this knowledge to understand and solve national social problems.

Another new development was the expansion of teaching of psychology in various professional courses in the fields of engineering, agriculture, management, and medical sciences. All five Indian Institutes of Technology have Departments of Humanities and Social Sciences of which psychology is a constituent subject with doctoral programmes. All four Indian Institutes of Management have the Departments of Organizational Behaviour. Psychology is taught in undergraduate classes, particularly in Home Science and Extension Education Departments in 26 agricultural universities and 28 agriculture institutes. In medical colleges, psychology is a part of a course on Preventive and Social Medicine. As noted by Atal (1976), most of these courses in agriculture and medical colleges are taught by junior staff, research assistants, and demonstrators and are accorded low priority. The situation has not changed even today.

The expansion of psychology departments within the university system continued in the 1970s. However, it was becoming increasingly difficult to conduct research in the university departments. In the bureaucratic university setup, there was little organizational support for pursuing research projects. Again, due to the mass entry of students seeking higher education and chronic campus unrest for political reasons, the academic environment was rapidly deteriorating. The heavy teaching load and no incentive for research had a telling effect on the research output of universities. As a result, research in psychology began to be conducted outside the university system. Psychologists with a research orientation preferred to join various research institutes. The ANS Institute of Social Studies, Patna, the Centre for the Study of Developing Societies, Delhi, and the National Institute of Community Development, Hyderabad, are examples of some such prominent institutes which became centres of research in psychology.

Many governmental and autonomous institutions, such as the National Council of Educational Research and Training (NCERT), the National Institute of Educational Policy and Administration (NIEPA), the National Institute of Public Cooperation and Child Development (NIPCCD), the National Institute of Health and Family Welfare (NIHFW)—(all in Delhi)—the Indian Institute of Science, Bangalore, Academic Staff College, Hyderabad, and the Indian Statistical Institute, Calcutta, have become centres of applied research in different fields of psychology. There are a large number of national and international voluntary agencies which seek services of psychologists to carry out research and field projects (see Table 4.1).

Table 4.1

Major Markers in the History of Psychology in India

Year	*Marker*
1905	First psychology laboratory in the philosophy department at Calcutta University
1916	First psychology department at Calcutta University
1924	Establishment of the Indian Psychological Association
1925	Launching of the Indian Journal of Psychology
1940	Founding of Lumbini Park Mental Hospital at Calcutta
1946	Establishment of the Institute of Psychological Research and Services
1956	Establishment of the University Grants Commission an agency responsible for the rapid expansion of psychology in universities and colleges
1962	Directorate of Psychological Research established by the Ministry of Defence
1969	Establishment of the Indian Council of Social Science Research—a major funding agency for psychological Research
1972	First Survey of Research in Psychology in India

Source: Sinha (1986).

Major Research Trends

It is an impossible task to document all the important research contributions made by Indian psychologists over the last 80 years. Sinha (1986), Dalal (1990) and the three ICSSR surveys of research in psychology have documented in detail the research efforts of Indian psychologists. Here, however, only the major research trends will be highlighted. The major streams of research, experiment, and testing continued to grow after Independence. Experimental work in the areas of perception, learning, and memory was primarily limited to replications of Western studies. Some good long-term research programmes were conducted. For almost two decades, Chatterjee (1954) conducted experiments on the role of intensity, time interval, and distance between stimuli in producing an optimal apparent movement. Tayal (1970) proposed a broad unifying 'model which could explain a number of related visual phenomena in terms of a new set of principles, challenging the theoretical basis of Fechner's law, in the area of verbal conditioning'. Das (1962) proposed that semantic satiation was a direct function of attentional decrement rather than of inhibition of meaning. Kothurkar (1972) conducted a series of studies on verbal learning and memory processes. Experimental work in comparative psychology was pioneered by Singh (1963) who studied the social behaviour of rhesus monkeys.

Research in the area of psychological testing made a quantum leap after Independence. The orientation was predominantly British. Those who could go abroad for graduate training generally went to London and Edinburgh (Barnett, 1955). They were trained in the mental testing traditions of Spearman and Thomson. On their return, these psychologists were preoccupied with the assessment of intelligence and in adapting Spearman, Binet-Simon, Stanford-Binet, and Terman-Merrill scales in Indian languages. A large number of Christian missionaries were also involved in the construction and validation of psychological tests for their mission schools (Mitra, 1972). In his presidential address to the Vth Annual Convention of the National Academy of Psychology, Puhan (1995) critically reviewed the history of personality test movement in India.

Work in the early stages in this area dealt with the construction and standardization of achievement and intelligence tests, aptitude scales, and personality inventories. Many popular Western tests were adapted in Indian languages. The NCERT reviewed all the tests that had been prepared up to 1961 (NCERT, 1968). A large number of these tests were adaptations of Western tests. Pareek and Rao (1974a) compiled a directory of Indian tests in different areas. It is interesting to note that out of 503 tests, 218 were in the area of personality. In the area of personality, one out of five tests assessed motivational variables. Even among those grouped into the general category, a large number were multidimensional personality tests, or measures of one or more motivational variables. Motivational tests were primarily in the domains of achievement motivation, anxiety, level of aspiration, and self-concept.

A few general observations can be made for the majority of these tests. First, most of the tests required certain language skills and thus were appropriate only for urban, educated samples. Half of the tests listed by Pareek and Rao (1974a) were for school and college-level students. Second, classical psychometric theory guided the construction of almost all these tests which, owing to subcultural and language difference, merit a fresh look at their usefulness. Third, there has been a general tendency to overlook the validity of these tests. More than 85 per cent of the tests listed by Pareek and Rao had no information on test validity.

Thus, though a large number of tests were developed in India, their quality left much to be desired. *The Handbook of Tests* prepared by Pestonjee (1986) revealed considerable improvement in the tests. All the 326 tests developed in the preceding decade followed the same trend as seen in the handbook prepared by Pareek and Rao but there were two differences. First, more than 60 per cent of the tests were reported with validity data, and second, there were more Indian tests and less adaptation of Western tests.

A large number of surveys were undertaken to investigate the prevalence of mental health problems by Sethi and his associates (Sethi, Gupta, and Kumar, 1967; Sethi et al., 1972) in Lucknow, by Dube (1984) in Agra, by Elnagar, Mittra, and Rao (1971) in rural Bengal, and by Verghese (1973) in Vellore. There were very few in-depth studies of the problem areas. Research in the areas of epidemiology of mental illness, phenomenology of depressive behaviour, drug abuse, yoga and health, psychosocial aspects of family planning, and mental retardation slowly gathered momentum by the 1970s (Prabhu, 1980). In the area of clinical psychology, most of the research activities were confined to diagnosis and prognosis of mental diseases. Wig and Akhtar (1974) have reviewed important psychiatric research conducted during 1947–72 in India. Murthi (1980) observed that Western influence was significant in the use of clinical techniques, such as sensitization, aversion therapy, feedback therapy, and classical and operant conditioning techniques in the treatment of psychogenic illnesses. Behaviour therapies were quite popular and though psychoanalysis continued to be practised, its popularity was on the decline. Recently, psychologists have evinced a keen interest in examining traditional healing practices in the treatment of mental illnesses (Kakar, 1982). One area which has attracted attention of late is health psychology (Dalal, 1995), that is, the role of psychological and cultural factors in affecting health behaviour.

An applied area that began to draw the attention of scholars after Independence was industrial psychology. Rapid industrialization in the 1950s and 1960s created the need for better understanding of the labour–management relationship and organizational efficiency. Psychological research studies on job attitude, work incentive, absenteeism, and job satisfaction were widely popular till the 1970s. Ganguli's (1961) book illustrates the concerns of that period. Following the introduction of many self-employment schemes by the central government in the 1960s, the research focus shifted to developing training programmes for inculcating entrepreneurship. McClelland's (1961) theory of achievement motivation provided the basis for conducting a unique experiment to impart training for achievement at the Small Industries Extension Training Institute, Hyderabad. The findings of this innovative training were not conclusive, and eventually Indian psychologists lost interest in such experimentation.

With the shift in research from industrial to organizational behaviour, there was an interest in studying all aspects of organized work activities. Research on the influence of socio-economic factors and traditional culture on organizational functioning began to engage the attention of Indian psychologists. In the Third Survey, two chapters on job attitudes (Padaki, 1988) and on organizational effectiveness (Khandwalla, 1988) cover a large number of Indian studies in these areas.

Communal and caste conflicts being perennial problems in India, social prejudice, intergroup relations, and socialization of the Indian child emerged as major research interests. Rath and Sircar (1960) and Anant (1970) studied caste stereotypes. Paranjpe's (1970) book was based on a survey of college students' prejudice against low-caste members. The studies of attitude toward the Chinese (Sinha and Upadhyaya, 1960) are oft-quoted studies of change in attitude as a result of historical events (border dispute with China which led to war). Singh (1981) studied the development of religious identity and prejudice in children, and Deridder and Tripathi (1992) examined the social consequences of norm violation by different ethnic groups. Research in the field of socialization and child-rearing practices in India is also substantial. Two field studies, which inspired many studies of the early period, are by a British, Carstairs (1957) and two Americans, Minturn and Hitchcock (1966). Work on similar lines has been done by Anandlakshmy (1975, 1982) and others. Kakar (1978) examined socialization and child rearing in light of the adolescence. Elaborate system of rituals and practices prevalent in Hindu culture. Saraswathi (1987) and Varma (1976) reported studies on moral development, much along the lines of Kohlberg's work.

To take stock of the state of research, Ganguli (1971) reviewed around 2,000 research publications of the period from 1920 to 1967. He found that five areas of work in order of their importance were social (15.9%), experimental (13.7%), mental testing (13.0%), general (10.6%), and industrial (3.6%). A review of publications by Mitra (1972) revealed that clinical, social, personality, and experimental areas accounted for half of the total number of publications reviewed.

By the mid-1970s, a crisis of identity in Indian psychology was imminent. The enthusiasm which the Western-educated Indian psychologists carried along with their degrees was waning. Indian scholars became restive as Western psychology failed to shed light on Indian social issues. Sixty years of Western psychology in India had not yielded any significant discoveries. As Nandy (1974) argued, 'Indian psychology has become not merely imitative and subservient but also dull and replicative' (p. 5). Agrawal (1973) called psychology in India as adaptology. There was a growing disillusionment with the applicability of Western theories and their mindless testing in India. Their failure to resolve inner conflicts of cherishing Indian cultural values at the personal level and maintaining high standards of objectivity at the professional level was reflected in their methodologically sophisticated but socially irrelevant research. Western psychological theories and research were not effective in understanding the Indian social reality. As a result, Indian psychologists became increasingly marginalized in society. A strong need was felt to return to the cultural roots. Sinha (1977) urged that the scientific understanding of Indian social reality should benefit from its vast treasure house of traditional psychological knowledge accumulated over centuries. He called for the development of an indigenous psychology with its own paradigms to understand the developmental problems of the region. In short, psychology in India was seeking its own identity.

This debate resulted in some noticeable change in the content and quality of Indian research. Indian psychologists evinced an increasing interest in studying problems relevant to the country using Indian concepts and theories. Neki (1973), for example, advocated the teacher–pupil model in clinical counselling to break down cultural and social barriers. J.B.P. Sinha (1980) proposed a new leadership style (nurturant task leader) that is more likely to succeed in Indian work organizations. Kakar (1982b, 1991) examined the role of traditional healers in maintaining mental health in traditional societies. Rao (1983) and Palsane et al. (1986) developed a concept of stress based on ancient scriptures. Pande and Naidu (1992) developed a measure to study the concept of detachment and its consequences on mental health.

However, these efforts to investigate indigenous concepts and theories were fragmented and did not show any long-term research commitment. It is heartening to find research studies using Indian concepts, but such attempts are largely one-time affair lacking in-depth analysis. The best examples of long-term thematic research have employed Western models (Kanekar, 1988; Singh, 1986; Singh and Singh, 1994). Relevant in this context is the fact that major funding agencies play an important role in setting the priority areas of the research endeavours. The UGC, the NCERT, and the ICSSR in particular have shaped the nature and direction of research over the past four decades. A perusal of research projects sanctioned by the ICSSR shows that between 1969 and 1972, no research projects on tribal communities were funded whereas during 1982–85 and only 27 per cent of the projects financed were tribal studies, indicating the spurt of research in this area in the last decade.

The Third Survey of Research in Psychology (Pandey, 1988) presents a comprehensive picture of the contemporary research trends in India. Four major emerging trends in Indian research were identified: (i) outgrowing the alien (Western) framework, (ii) psychological assessment in the Indian sociocultural context, (iii) deriving researchable ideas from indigenous thought and traditions, and (iv) research for socio-economic change and national development. In addition, many new areas of research have emerged, such as cognitive development of school children, particularly language development (Mohanty, 1982); poverty, inequality, and social justice (Pareek, 1980); social psychology of crowding (Jain, 1978); manipulative social behaviour (Pandey, 1986); psychology of rural development (Muthayya, 1982); and causal attributions of achievement and social behaviour (Dalal, 1988).

Table 4.2

Number of Studies Using Different Types of Samples and Methods in Personality and Social Psychology Research from 1972 to 1986

Period	*Sample*				*Method n*		*Review Articles*	*Total*
	School	*College*	*Cohorts*	*General*	*Exp*	*Non-exp*		
Personality								
1972–76	85	67	29	34	51	164	25	240
	(39)	(31)	(13)	(16)	(24)	(76)	(10)	
1977–81	145	112	84	92	66	367	79	512
	(33)	(26)	(19)	(21)	(15)	(85)	(15)	
1982–86	183	108	131	99	82	439	172	693
	(35)	(21)	(25)	(19)	(16)	(84)	(20)	
Social								
1972–76	66	65	109	168	53	355	72	480
	(16)	(16)	(27)	(41)	(13)	(87)	(17)	
1977–81	96	134	152	233	79	536	461	1076
	(16)	(22)	(25)	(38)	(13)	(87)	(40)	
1982–86	99	124	127	193	75	468	566	1109
	(18)	(23)	(23)	(36)	(14)	(86)	(48)	

In general, as reported by Sinha (1993), clinical, social, personality, and industrial organizational areas accounted for 70 per cent of all publications. The rate of growth of research publications was 5.57 per cent in the 1950s, 14.28 per cent in the 1960s, and 46.22 per cent in the 1970s. Dalal and Sharma (1990) examined the growth pattern of research for the period 1972–86 by content analysing the abstracts included in the *Indian Psychological Abstracts* in the areas of social psychology and personality.

It is interesting to note that in the initial period (1972–76) one-fourth of all studies adopted the experimental method to investigate personality; this, however, declined in later years. In social psychology, only 13 per cent utilized the experimental method and this figure remained constant in the following years. In the area of personality, there were an increasingly large number of theoretical papers, whereas in social psychology, the questionnaire method became popular over the years. Using samples of student population in these research studies was far less than that found in Western research (see Table 4.2).

Teaching Programmes

Graduate training in psychology is provided by 67 Indian universities. Besides, it is taught in nearly 1,400 colleges and other institutions. Teaching programmes in most of these universities still follow the British pattern. The postgraduate programme is of two years duration, in which students are required to take from three to five courses each year with practical work involving laboratory experiments and testing. A master's degree is a prerequisite for admission to the PhD programme. For a doctoral degree, students are under a senior faculty member and write a dissertation. Some universities now give MPhil as an intermediary research degree.

The UGC Report (1968) lists the courses offered at the graduate level in 30 universities. The compulsory and elective courses, in order of their frequencies of universities offering them, are listed in Table 4.3. Social psychology was the most popular course taught in 23 universities compared to the other seven courses taught as electives. While, all other compulsory courses were academic in nature, the elective courses such as industrial, educational, guidance, and clinical are of applied nature. The UGC Report (1968) recommended that applied courses should emphasize fieldwork in active collaboration with the concerned agencies. In practice, practical training was imparted only in the area of clinical and industrial psychology, that too in selective universities. Other places it is merely as a classroom course.

A decade later, the UGC appointed a panel to formulate guidelines for reorienting the teaching of psychology at the graduate level. Four regional workshops were held at Baroda, Mysore, Allahabad, and Bhubaneswar for this purpose. The UGC

Panel (Rath, 1979) made several valuable recommendations. It suggested the introduction of professional courses with practical training and work experience, diploma courses for imparting job-oriented specialization in different fields, and sound training in research methodology.

Table 4.3

Rank Order of Courses Taught at Master's Level in Indian University

In 1966		*In 1984*	
Compulsory	*Elective*	*Compulsory*	*Elective*
Social	Industrial	Research methods	Industrial organizational behaviour
General	Educational	Social	Clinical
Experimental	Guidance	Experimental	Educational
Research methods	Clinical	Psychological testing	Counselling
History	Psychological testing	Abnormal	Guidance
Psychological testing	Comparative	Physiological	Personality
Physiological	Criminology	System and theories	Psychological testing

The data compiled by the UGC (1985) revealed that some of the suggestions were indeed implemented by various university departments, though there was no radical departure from the past. The courses offered most often are listed in rank order in Table 4.3. It can be seen that compulsory courses in 1966 and 1984 were more or less the same, except that general psychology and history of psychology were included at the undergraduate level. Almost all the universities offered courses on research methodology. Elective courses, such as industrial, clinical, and educational psychology continued to be included in the second year curriculum of master's degree in most of the universities. However, instead of industrial psychology, organizational behaviour, and personnel psychology courses became increasingly popular. Comparative psychology and criminology which were previously taught in 17 universities lost their prominence and did not figure in the list. It may be interesting to note that a course on Indian psychology which was offered at eight universities in 1966 was not taught in any of the universities in 1984. This course evolved around ancient Indian thought and concepts and was incompatible with the ethos of scientific psychology. The new courses which were offered were biopsychology (Gujarat), behavioural genetics (Calcutta), cognitive processes (Calcutta, Osmania, Poona, and Allahabad), psychology of disadvantaged children (Utkal), and social change (Allahabad).

In general, most of these courses and teaching programmes in psychology are academic in nature, with little field training. Psychology courses have not been modified over time. As a result, these courses are not very popular among bright students, who seek professional courses. Traditional psychology courses do not provide training in skills necessary to compete in the job market. This has led to a paradoxical situation of unemployment and unemployability of students of psychology who have completed their postgraduate and doctoral programmes. The earlier recommendations of the UGC Panel (Rath, 1979) regarding job-oriented diploma courses did not make much headway. Again, in 1995, the UGC Panel in Psychology appointed a committee headed by J. Pandey, which identified the areas in which undergraduate and postgraduate level diploma courses could be funded by the UGC. Many psychology departments are seriously considering the possibility of introducing new professional programmes in clinical psychology, counselling, human resource development, and community development. This shift in thinking is inevitable with the existing courses becoming irrelevant in the light of the new economic policy of the government.

One of the major handicaps in the study of psychology is the acute dearth of good textbooks in Hindi and other regional languages. Books in regional languages are poor adaptations/translations of popular Western textbooks; even examples quoted therein are from Western settings which an average Indian student finds hard to appreciate. This has a dampening effect on sustaining interest in the study of psychology. In the absence of good textbooks by Indian authors, the research done in India is not disseminated to the classroom level. There are no good Indian textbooks in the applied field either. Of late, a lot of concern has been expressed about this, but the teaching of psychology in India continues to be divorced from the social reality in the country.

State of the Profession

The prime national body of psychologists, the Indian Psychological Association is now 70 years old. Its official journal, the *Indian Journal of Psychology* had played an important role in shaping the discipline during its formative years. However, the association has steadily declined and has lost its Indian character, mainly due to personal rivalry among the senior members, and due to power politics and litigations. This has resulted in widespread alienation among Indian psychologists, so much so that less than one per cent of around 4,500 psychologists are members of the Indian Psychological Association. The electoral roll for the 1991 election showed a total membership of 251, of which 234 were life members. The problems confronting the association are reflected in the irregular and poor-quality articles published in its official journal. In 1989, the National Academy of Psychology was established to promote professional activities. Despite a good start, this body has yet to make a mark on the growth of psychology in the country.

Other professional bodies such as the Indian Psychoanalytic Society, the Indian Association of Clinical Psychologists, and the Indian Academy of Applied Psychology have been functioning irregularly. Among the regional and state-level associations, the Madras Psychological Society, the Kerala Psychological Association, and the Bombay Psychological Association are intermittently active; they organize their conventions and/or publish their journals. The functioning of these professional bodies is so much personalized that their activities are largely dependent on the interest and commitment of the office bearers.

The same is true of journal publication. According to a list prepared earlier (Dalal, 1990), 44 psychology journals are published in India. Many new ones have been launched since then. The fact is that bringing out a journal is often one-person show—the editor is responsible for reviewing, editing, and publication work. There is rarely a consistent review policy or a professional body supporting a journal. Nevertheless, journal publication is a popular professional activity in India. Some journals which are doing relatively well are as follows: *Indian*

Journal of Applied Psychology, Indian Journal of Clinical Psychology, Indian Journal of Social Work, Manosamiksha, Psychological Studies, Social Change, Indian Journal of Current Psychological Researches, Indian Journal of Personality and Clinical Psychology, Journal of Indian Academy of Applied Psychology, and *Social Engineer.* The *NIMHANS Journal, Journal of Indian Psychology,* and *Psychology and Developing Societies* are acclaimed to have some international standard.

To obtain a demographic profile of Indian psychologists, Pareek, Dixit, and Saruparіya (1979) mailed questionnaires to 2,500 psychologists, of which 589 were returned. Analysis revealed that 43.5 per cent of all psychologists had doctoral degree, and 9.5 per cent of them had obtained their degrees from universities abroad, mostly from USA, Canada, and Britain. A majority of the psychologists with foreign degrees were working in research institutions. Most of those who had a doctoral degree from Indian universities were working in the university setup; college teachers normally had a postgraduate degree. The data further revealed that very few psychologists were in applied and administrative jobs. Furthermore, about 90 per cent of the psychologists were working in larger towns and only between three and four per cent in rural areas. An analysis of the psychologists' biodata, as given in a subsequent directory (Nijhawan, 1983), revealed a somewhat similar trend. A majority of the psychologists listed in the directory had a doctoral degree (52.2%) and about 12 per cent had studied abroad (for master's or doctoral degree). Apart from a few who were working in service organizations, most of them were in academic institutions, and none were working in rural areas. It is quite possible that only a few psychologists outside the academia could be contacted to prepare the directory. In any case there is clear evidence that psychology in India is overwhelmingly an urban discipline. This fact is evident from a more recent computerized directory of psychologists (ICSSR, 1994), who were without exception working in the urban areas.

The areas of specialization of Indian psychologists coded from the data obtained in 1968, 1983, and 1994 are presented in Table 4.4. The data were compiled from different sources and should not be taken as conclusive. Furthermore, Indian psychologists often tend to change their area of specialization. Nevertheless, some patterns are clearly discernible in Table 4.4. In 1968, 31 per cent of the psychologists were working in the field of general psychology, this figure declined to 3.7 per cent in 1983, and in 1994 no psychologists were working in this area. The most popular area of study in 1983 was educational psychology; in 1994 it was industrial and organizational psychology, followed by social psychology. The fields of testing, personality, clinical, and educational psychology continued to be the most popular study areas. The content analysis of the 1994 directory further revealed that rural, health, and cross-cultural psychologies were emerging as the new areas of interest.

Table 4.4

Indian Psychologists and Their Major Areas of Research Interests

Area	*1968 (n = 734)**		*1983 (n = 356)***		*1994 (n = 105)****	
	%	*Rank*	*%*	*Rank*	*%*	*Rank*
General	30.8	1	3.7	9	–	–
Clinical/ Abnormal	13.2	2	7.0	5	46.7	3
Social	8.3	3	8.4	3	47.6	2
Educational	8.1	4	11.2	1	35.2	6
Industrial/ Organization	6.3	5	4.5	7	63.8	1
Personality	5.1	6	9.3	2	42.9	4
Vocational guidance	4.9	7	4.2	8	8.6	9
Child developmental	4.6	8	7.3	–	38.0	5
Experimental	3.0	9		4	23.8	8
Psychometric/ Testing	1.9	10	5.1	6	30.5	7
Rural/Tribal	–	11	3.4	10	6.7	10

Notes: *Data reproduced from S.C. Mitra (1972)
** Compiled from the National Register of Social Scientists (1983).
*** Data content analysed from the ICSSR Directory (1994). Multiple specializations were reported by each psychologist.

It may also be mentioned that psychology in India is more popular among female students. As a result, a large majority of students enrolled in the master's programme are females. In 1980–81, the total number of students enrolled in psychology was 4,194 (Sinha, 1986), of which 65 per cent were females. The number of female students further increased to 71 per cent in 1982–83. This is neither due to a chance, nor a passing fad, as confirmed by Prabhu (1983) in the field of clinical psychology particularly. In a survey, Singh and Dalal (1988) found that 53 per cent of the doctoral candidates in their national sample were females. Poor job prospects and fascination for clinical-counselling work could be the probable reasons for this.

Whither Psychology

As mentioned earlier, the crisis of identity and the growing realization of the futility of imitative psychological research led to some serious thinking in the 1970s about the future of psychology. What will make it more relevant in the Indian context? In the concluding chapter of the Second Survey of Research in Psychology, Pareek (1981) argued that psychology in India was standing at the 'crossroads'. He discussed many referents of relevance such as conceptual, methodological, professional, sociocultural, and the capability of the discipline to respond to societal needs. There are not many pointers that the situation had changed since then. Sinha (1986) also stressed the need to search for appropriate theoretical framework and research methodology to make the subject 'socially relevant to meet the needs of a changing society' (p. 63). Janak Pandey (1988) in the *Third Survey of Research in Psychology*, responding to Pareek's comment, concluded that 'psychology is outgrowing the alien models and ... probably psychology is not standing at the cross-roads' (p. 354). It seems that despite the optimism expressed from time to time, psychological research in India has not taken any discernible direction so far.

J.B.P. Sinha (1993) drew a distinction between the bulk and the front of psychological research. Not much has changed in the mass produced bulk of the research which continues to be replicative and imitative. However, as a consequence of the long debate, some criss-crossing streams in psychological research arc identifiable among the front runners. These are search for cultural significates, problem orientation, cross-cultural research, and indigenization.

The main thrust of a number of studies in the first stream is to identify the unique features of Indian culture and to demonstrate, empirically and through scriptures, that the Western concepts and theories are not applicable to the Indian cultural reality. The cultural significates are identified by contrasting Indian and Western perspectives. Based on the content analysis of stories from school textbooks, Kakar (1971) noted that the image of authority was either nurturant or assertive, but never impersonal or fraternal. Festinger's position that cognitive dissonance leads to stress was questioned, suggesting that in the Indian mind opposites coexist without any attempt to synthesize them. The integration takes place within a philosophical system at a higher level of abstraction. Tripathi (1988) contrasted models of men in the Indian and Western traditions. Comparing Indian and Western assumptions about self, consciousness, and nature, Paranjpe (1984) highlighted the similarities and differences. Agrawal and Misra (1986, 1990) demonstrated that the goals and means which define achievements in the Indian sociocultural context were different from those found in the West. In their studies social concern-related goals accounted for maximum variance.

The emphasis on problem-oriented research began around the same time. The proposition was that psychological research must not be merely an academic exercise but must have practical utility. Many theoretical developments held the promise of applying psychological knowledge to the Indian setting. The main argument was that the research should focus on the study of problems facing the country. Psychological knowledge should contribute to solving the problems of a developing society. Reviewing relevant Indian studies, Sinha (1973) examined the methodological difficulties of conducting problem-oriented research. Studies of political behaviour (Mehta, 1975), developmental norms for preschool children (Murlidharan, 1971), change in the level of aspiration and motivation of farmers (Sinha, 1969), prolonged deprivation (Misra, 1982), and health modernity (Singh, 1983) are some examples of such research. Pareek and Rao (1974b) reviewed research in the field of family planning and proposed a conceptual model of fertility regulating behaviour. This interest in studying Indian problems is clearly reflected in a number of later studies. It was also realized that Western theories and methods could not be fruitfully applied to the study of Indian social problems. In the absence of cumulative knowledge based on cultural understanding and field testing, these studies did not yield any real insight and solutions to the problems. Indian social problems demanded indigenous solutions.

A parallel development was cross-cultural testing of psychological concepts and theories. For Indian psychologists who had an international orientation, it was an opportunity to operate on a wider plane and to influence developments in mainstream psychology. Cross-cultural movement found natural patronage in India and a large number of Indian psychologists joined this international movement. They occupied important positions in the International Association of Cross-Cultural Psychology and played a prominent role in augmenting this movement. However, as noted by Sinha (1996a), cross-cultural work only led to testing of Western theories on Indian samples. Rarely did studies originate from the needs of Indian society or tested Indian concepts in other cultures. Indiscriminate search for cultural differences and similarities made such ventures superficial, and they did not enhance one's understanding of Indian culture or the contemporary problems of Indian society. To a large extent cross-cultural psychology remained a methodological enterprise and culture remained a peripheral concern (Misra and Gergen, 1993). In recent years cross-cultural psychology itself is going through a crisis and the classical conception of culture which was the basis of most researches in this area is being questioned (Miller, 1996).

The fourth development, a major one, was that of psychology becoming more indigenous. At the core of indigenization was the belief that all knowledge including psychology is rooted in the prevalent worldview of the community and is conditioned by historical and sociocultural factors. Sinha (1994) discussed in detail the indigenization of psychology in India, and two facets of indigenization. First is purely the product of culture, the concepts and categories which are culture-bound. Second is the product of the interaction of cultural variables with concepts, theories, and methods introduced from outside. Sinha cited a large number of

Indian studies in support of Indian psychology becoming indigenous.

Adair, Puhan, and Vohra (1993) provided some empirical data to ascertain the extent of indigenization of psychology in India. Indigenization was operationalized in terms of the following: (i) cultural sensitivity of research in designing a study and discussing its findings, (ii) citations from own culture, (iii) problem orientation, (iv) development of culture-based concepts, theories, and methods, (v) culturally anchored tests, and (vi) cross-cultural comparisons. They sampled 74, 129, and 153 research articles from leading Indian journals for the periods 1972–74, 1978–80, and 1984–87 and concluded that indigenization of the discipline was slow, though signs of its emergence were evident. Sinha (1993) expressed doubts about indigenization of psychology in India. He argued, '... indigenous theories, concepts, and methods are too few to give Indian psychology an authentic identity of its own' (p. 8). Sinha posited that the creative efforts of a majority of front runners were directed in varying degrees toward different ways of integrative indigenization, referring to appropriate rather than narrowly defined 'indigenous psychology'. Transplanting a concept from an alien culture, or studying an indigenous concept using an alien methodology has often been an unproductive exercise. A large body of research cited as blazing a trail of indigenization is in reality indigenous only in terms of concepts. The research ethos, problem formulation, methodology, and data analysis follow the same process as any imitative Western research. Despite all pleas, promises, and provocations such indigenous researches failed to enthuse Indian researchers beyond producing an occasional publication. There was no thematic long-term indigenous research programme.

Psychology in India in Search of an Identity

The front runners among Indian psychologists did respond to the dominance of Western psychology by initiating research in new directions, that is, along the four streams discussed earlier. These research activities raised the hope that psychology in India is eventually arriving and is better prepared to deal with the complexities of a rapidly changing social world; to understand the meaning and psychosocial consequences of the opening up of the

Indian economy. In a seminar on Psychology as a Policy Science, held at Allahabad, Tripathi (1989) claimed that psychologists in India are better placed today than ever before to play a more active role in formulating policies and various schemes of poverty alleviation. Such confidence shown by Indian psychologists is indicative of their earnest desire to broad base the psychological inquiry. As a policy science, psychologists would be expected to provide the knowledge base to assist policy planners in the decision-making process. It is the responsibility of psychologists to shape public opinion by informing people of the challenges and dangers of unprecedented technological advances. They have a role in facilitating smooth transformation of the developing society. In order to achieve these goals, there is a need for major paradigm shift in psychological research.

However, Indian psychologists are troubled by the incompatibility of these expectations with the present state of the discipline. The replicative nature of their research endeavour antiquated and outdated teaching programmes, and lack of applied orientation have failed to provide any professional momentum to the discipline. Indian psychologists do not feel that they are part of the present social transformation. They want to break free from theoretical and methodological constraints of the discipline to grapple with the real issue of development and to act as social catalysts in the change process. They are also aware that if they fail to meet the challenge, they may get completely marginalized. There are both endogenous and exogenous pressures to seek an identity for the discipline which is in tune with the present national concerns.

Psychology in India needs an impact evaluation to ascertain the ways it has influenced people's lives. This impact evaluation needs to be in terms of enhancement of public awareness of psychological concepts and theories, applications of research in the developmental schemes, role of psychologists as social activists and policy planners, citation of Indian research, research funding, indigenization, etc. Systematic impact evaluations should replace impressionistic appraisals of psychology in India. Such impact evaluation should also throw light on the cost which psychology in India has paid for pursuing Western research. It appears that Indian psychologists were always conscious of the fact that such research pursuits would not enhance their understanding of Indian social reality. The Indian experience has little parallel in Western societies and its complexities could not be encompassed by the linear and ahistorical Western models. Thus, there was little meaning in applying this body of knowledge to the Indian setting. Academic research became an end in itself. It developed its own ethos, support system, and self-serving research programmes. It is not surprising that psychology students earnestly scan books and journals in libraries, particularly *Psychological Abstracts,* to find their research problem, unmindful of the real life problems they experience in everyday life. This mindset perpetuates throughout their career. There are only occasional insightful studies which stand out. Largely, Indian psychologists create their own world and priorities which do not overlap with the real world outside. They continue to live in two parallel worlds, while investing their creative energy in activities other than their professional ones.

This mental frame of the majority of Indian psychologists is clearly reflected in the declining quality of research publications. The bulk of the research activities were only half-hearted efforts which rarely sustained over a longer period of time. Instances of thematic long-term research programmes are few. It appears that Indian psychologists did not respect their own research, not to speak of the research of their colleagues. This is one of the reasons why no research traditions were built up which could be passed from one generation to the other. Very often colleagues in the same institution are not aware of each other's research work, while they are quite enlightened about the work of their Western counterparts. This mutual disrespect for each other's work is also evident in the sorry state of professional bodies and journal publications.

One may ask the following questions: Why did Indian psychologists not change the content of their research to make it relevant to the Indian context? Why do they continue to engage in research which is implicative and an extension of Western work in the Indian setting? What are the psychological compulsions of Indian psychologists? Is it possible that the kind of professional training they receive does not prepare them to deal with larger social issues? Why are they wary of venturing out of the narrow disciplinary boundaries? Are they afraid of losing their identity as scientists in venturing out of the narrow disciplinary boundaries?

Why is there minimal input from Indian cultural traditions in research and teaching? It needs to be investigated why in spite of repeated pleas indigenization is not evident in Indian studies. These questions demand in-depth analysis.

There is a growing realization that the distinct identity of psychology in India is contingent upon its cultural identity, that is, on culturally grounded psychological theories. This requires a different view of knowledge and methods of its acquisition. Behaviour needs to be understood not only in terms of individual emotions and thought processes but also, and more importantly, within the context of the family, the community, and other social collectives in which the individual is embedded.

Indian society is witnessing rapid and continuous transformation. With the policy of economic liberalization, the country is opening up to all kinds of global influences. The breakthroughs in telecommunications and visual media have overcome barriers of geographical distances. As a result of the global influences, there is continuous blending, appropriation, dissolution, and reconstruction of cultural elements. Against this backdrop, search for stable pattern and long range predictions cannot be the goal of psychological inquiry. Psychology as a viable science is concerned with identifying those mechanisms that lie at the interface between culture and the individual and locating how cultural processes become psychological processes and vice versa. Indian culture is heterogeneous comprising diverse ethnic groups. There is enough potential for testing indigenously developed theories within the broader Indian cultural traditions.

The viability of psychology as a cultural science is contingent upon a more dynamic definition of culture itself. The classical definition of culture in cross-cultural research (Berry, 1980) views culture as a stable state which can be used as an explanatory concept. Culture and psychology are viewed as two separate entities influencing each other. In the new conceptualization, culture and psychology are viewed as integral to each other. In the changing scenario, cultural traditions are also undergoing a change as manifested in the psychological processes (Shweder, 1991). As far as the outside influences become part of the cultural experience, they are legitimate subject matter for the cultural science of psychology. This open boundary approach to culture is consistent with the plural Indian tradition and is essential to make sense of the rapid social changes.

In this pursuit, the role of Indian psychologists has to undergo a major change. Pareek (1981) argued that as members of a society, their concern for social issues and commitment to some basic values and social goals is important. Value-free position is a myth and self-deception. The question of cultural relevance of the discipline cannot be divorced from the commitment of its members to some societal values. For example, spiritual values which are ingrained in the psyche of Indians cannot be ignored in the name of secular scientific research. Misra and Gergen (1993) stated that the role of psychologist as a knowledgeable person would be to help in understanding, reading, and interpreting behavioural episodes within the culture, and informing people about the potentialities of action within the range of possibilities in a culture. Thus, the researcher would be a co-participant in the joint construction of reality, rather than an authority to control and predict the future of a person (p. 237).

Indian psychologists can no longer remain distant observers behind the walls of professional neutrality. Their two worlds, professional and personal, can meet only when research issues spring from their heart and psychological inquiry defines their own existence within a culture. The emergence of psychology as a cultural science appears to be a real possibility as psychology in India enters into the twenty first century.

5

Social Construction of Knowledge

The Case of Research in Psychology in India

Indian scriptures, dating back thousands of years, extensively dealt with the analysis of states of consciousness and contents of mental activities. The important feature of this early exposition is that it is mostly experiential and is a culmination of centuries-old tradition of self-verification. In the ancient Indian scriptures no rigid distinction among religion, philosophy, and psychology was maintained. The overriding consideration was to help individuals in their pursuit of self-realization and liberation from the miseries of life. In this worldview, the source of all suffering was presumed to be within the person, and thus the emphasis was on exploring the 'world within' to alleviate the suffering. The goal was to seek enduring harmony of spirit, mind, and body for everlasting happiness. The yoga system evolved very sophisticated mind-control techniques in this pursuit. In contemporary literature this broad field of inquiry is referred to as 'Indian psychology'.

These rich traditions, however, had little bearing on academic psychology implanted in India as a Western science during the British rule. Scientific psychology with laboratory work was a novel approach, not having any parallel in traditional

Indian psychology. Psychology was first introduced as a subject in the philosophy department at Calcutta University. Brojendra Nath Seal who was the then King George V Professor of Mental and Moral Philosophy at the University of Calcutta drafted the first syllabus for experimental psychology and established a laboratory for demonstration purpose in 1905. Eleven years later, this laboratory was upgraded as the first psychology department, the Department of Experimental Psychology. Narendra Nath Sengupta, who had his education at the Harvard University, chaired this department. It may be interesting to note that the first university department was that of experimental psychology so as to align it with contemporary developments in European psychology on one hand and to completely dissociate it from Indian spiritual traditions on the other. Laboratory research at Calcutta in the areas of depth perception, psychophysics, and attention gave academic psychology the status of value-free, secular science. Recognizing the scientific nature of research, psychology was included as a separate section in the Indian Science Congress as early as in 1923, something which Western psychology achieved only after a long struggle.

Indian psychology has come a long way in the 100 years of its existence. Though the progress was very slow in the next four decades, particularly before the Independence, psychology departments were established only in two more universities at Mysore and Patna, before 1950. Twelve new psychology departments were established by 1950 and the number went up to 32 by the end of 1960s. Presently there are around 150 psychology departments at the university level. There is no authentic data about the number of psychology faculty in the country which official agencies, like the UGC or ICSSR, can furnish. One estimate (Jain, 2005) suggests that there were more than 15,000 psychologists in India. In any case, India has the largest number of psychologists outside the Western block, and was considered a 'publication giant' among all developing countries (Gilgin and Gilgin, 1987). This rapid expansion of the discipline has aroused many hopes and expectations about its possible contribution to the success of nation-building projects. The problems of poverty, illiteracy, urban decay, and disease control cannot be handled on the basis of sound economic planning only, but also require changes in the attitudes and beliefs of people, and their motivations for collective action. This calls for a realistic appraisal of the impediments which psychology in India is currently experiencing. Psychology needs to break its present disciplinary shackles to join hands with other social sciences. Currently, much soul-searching is going on within the discipline and it is realized that psychology in India needs to be rooted in its own history and heritage.

There are few reviews of research in the pre-Independence period. One was by Bose (1939) who reviewed the progress of the past 25 years. In the 1960s and onwards, a large number of such surveys came out. The surveys of research commissioned by ICSSR have brought out extensive reviews of research in psychology in India.

In recent years, there is a surge of several publications which enable critical evaluation of the development of psychology in India. Some of these writings (Dalal, 1990, 1996, 2002; Misra and Gergen, 1993; Sinha, 1986, 1996b; J.B.P. Sinha, 1993) have critically evaluated the progress of psychology). The five surveys of research in psychology (Mitra, 1972; Pareek, 1981, 1980; Misra, 2007; J. Pandey, 2004, 2001, 1988) covered important research contributions since the beginning of the last century. Pareek and Rao (1974a), Pestonjee (1986), and the NCERT (1981) compiled psychological measures developed in India. Reports prepared by the University Grants Commission (UGC, 1968, 1982, 1999) deal with teaching and research programmes in universities. Some empirical studies (Adair, 1990) have examined the professional status of the discipline of psychology. More recently, Misra (2005), Kumar (2005, 2008), Pandey and Singh (2005), Paranjpe (2006), and S. Varma (2004) have provided a broad overview of the research scenario and an incisive understanding of the current status of psychology in India. These reviews do impress a reader about the phenomenal growth of the discipline in India. They have basically dealt with the following: (i) developmental stages of psychology in India, (ii) enumerating research contributions of Indian psychologists, (iii) growth of psychology as a profession, and (iv) identifying emerging research trends. In dealing with these aspects, the emphasis was largely on portraying the state of psychology from the available data, without much consideration for the context. Such documentations and analysis imply a linear model of disciplinary growth; psychology progressing from one stage to another. The interface between science and society was rarely the subject matter of discussion.

Few efforts have been made in the past to establish linkages between the socialization of Indian psychologists and the state of the discipline. Kakar (1986) has postulated that Indian psychologists find it difficult to distance from their object of study (i.e. people), which their Western counterparts could easily do. They are not socialized to be impersonal and dispassionate in their observation of human behaviour. Kakar argued that for Indian psychologists relationship is more important than brute exposition of the truth. This causes an ambivalence and discomfort in pursuing human science as a relentless pursuit of scientific truth. Nandy (1995) examined the life and work of Girindra Shekhar Bose who introduced psychoanalysis in India. Nandy contended that for Bose, a typical Westernized upper class intellectual from Bengal, psychoanalysis served as a new instrument of social criticism and demystifying some aspects of Indian culture. Using it as a case in point, Nandy argued that the emerging intellectual culture under colonial influence had a significant bearing on the shaping of modern psychology.

Arguing along similar lines, Dalal (1996) has posited that Indian psychologists trained in the Western traditions lived in two parallel worlds. One was the world of academic psychology, with its own ethos, concerns and methodology. The objective, positivist approach to research provided legitimacy to their knowledge generation and sharing within the scientific community. To remain connected to the world outside they engaged in personally satisfying creative work compatible with their Indian upbringing. Thus, Indian scholars could remain staunch nationalists and social activists in their non-academic life, while pursuing Western science in India. This split-level consciousness was conducive to keeping social issues out of the academic agenda to a large extent. If at all, Indian social reality was observed through the tainted glasses of Western theories. Though the earlier passages provide a window into the mindset of Indian psychologists, the larger issues of science–society interface and the fashioning of psychology in India in twentieth century as an alien discipline are yet to be seriously looked into. We need to examine the social history and cultural ethos which shape intellectual climate and research agenda. Yogendra Singh (1986) has made an effort to critically examine the growth of sociology in India. He analysed the social conditioning of knowledge as revealed by the extent to which the concepts, methods and priority areas of research bear the imprints of history and social forces operative in society. Such an exercise is long overdue in the discipline of psychology. In recent years, social psychology of knowledge has emerged as a new field impregnated with many possibilities of examining social bases of knowledge. The present research endeavour is to employ its methodology to analyse modern psychology in India.

Social Psychology of Knowledge

With few exceptions, psychologists in the West modelled their epistemology, not on physical sciences per se but after the philosophy of physical sciences. Primed initially by nineteenth-century materialism, positivism, and realism, Western psychologists have exhibited their enduring commitment to search for the regularities in human behaviour and thinking. Psychological phenomena were treated on par with the physical phenomena having stable, universal characteristics. For example, psychologists always believed that the emotional states are empirical realities which can be observed and measured using the methods of physical sciences. The pursuit of psychological science was to unravel underlying universalities in human behaviour.

In recent decades the very definition of science is being seriously questioned. It is held that social science knowledge cannot be free from societal values and conditions within which it is generated. A new school of thought is emerging based on the premise that all knowledge about people and their social world is relative and context bound. Knowledge in this sense denotes shared realities of scientific communities holding similar beliefs and background. The proliferation of diverse and conflicting theoretical propositions and failure to unravel unifying principles, give credence to the argument that there is a close nexus between knowledge generation and scientific culture of the society. Recent developments in the emerging field of social psychology of knowledge have yielded many conceptual and methodological tools to examine social grounding of the knowledge.

The social psychology of knowledge has drawn from the diverse traditions of sociology of knowledge and social constructionism. The forerunner of these movements in the West is German philosopher Immanuel Kant who asserted that no scientific inquiry can be free from presuppositions. As Kant put it, no one can start from nothing; every mode of inquiry is equipped with a set of presuppositions, which are not subject to empirical testing. Building on this premise, sociology of knowledge emerged as a new field in the beginning of twentieth century. Its proponents, Sheler, Marx, Mannheim, and others questioned the modelling of social science epistemology after the philosophy of physical sciences. They pointed out that ideas and perceptions are not real in the sense of physical objects. These are the products of social processes and institutions, and belief system of a society. The problem of interrelationship between research ideas and social beliefs on one side, and finding observable social structures on the other side formulated the domain of sociology of knowledge. It is posited that society not only provides the context, but more importantly, shapes the nature of questions being asked in scientific inquiry also. Taking a more extreme position, many critics of science hold that scientific knowledge is a kind of belief system and sociology of knowledge is nothing but sociology of belief (Barnes, 1974).

Sociology of knowledge tries to relate the nature of social theory to the social position of the theorist. Taking this stance, Mannaheim (1940) argued that religion, occupation, age, gender, and similar categories have biasing effect on knowledge generation. To understand this biasing effect, it is important to juxtapose the conflicting modes of interpretations and then explore the perspectives with reference to each other. Mannheim brought out elaborate methodology to examine networks of relationship between science and society. Buss (1975), who dealt with the sociology of psychological knowledge, presented several examples of ways in which social and ideological factors have influenced various research trends in West. Paranjpe (1998) has employed Mannaheim's approach to compare Indian and Western perspectives and to examine the relationship between specific ideas and respective cultural perspectives.

The work of Mannheim, and that of Merton (1968) has led to a good deal of intellectual and evaluative debate about social distribution and social control of the modes of reality construction and of different types of constructs. Though criticized for its vagueness regarding sociology of scientific knowledge and 'absolute relativism', sociology of knowledge has brought to the forefront the sociocultural processes which shape the reality construction and the effects of the modes of reality construction on social structures, including academic institutions.

Extending this line of argument, a more recent approach to conceptualize knowledge in social sciences is that of social constructionism. The social constructionist approach contends that every researcher is a social product, who internalizes the value system of that society. These researchers bring to their work a stock of preconceived notions, comprising a network of propositions about human motivation, goals, and action patterns. From the constructionist point of view, knowledge is not an end product of scientific observations, rather observations are referents of the social world to which a scientist belongs. A constructionist emphasizes the social origins of the meanings of psychological concepts (Gergen, 1989b).

Social constructionists propose that knowledge does not exist independent of the social world of the knower. It is the social context that provides legitimacy and meaning to any knowledge. Thus, to understand the process of knowledge generation and its utilization one has to understand the knowledge base of that society. Social values, attitudes, behavioural norms, all modify description and interpretation of scientific observations. Bertrand Russell once said in jest about how the infrahuman subjects of British researchers were found to exhibit stereotypical British behaviour, while animals in American research acted in distinctly Yankee fashion (cited in Flanagan, 1981). Semin and Chassein (1985) established the dependency of formal and statistically derived models of personality structure on existing folk models of the mind.

Gergen (1994) has also made a distinction between modern and post-modern psychology. If modernist psychology is committed to knowable world, its universal properties are discovered through empirical methods, and hold a notion of research as progressive and knowledge as cumulative; for post-modernist the focus shifts to linguistic resources, context, culture, and social values as integral to the reality construction. The latter approach provides an opportunity to de-objectify the existing realities, to demonstrate their social and historical embeddedness, and to explore their implications for social life.

For this, psychologist is invited to conjoin personal, professional, and political perspectives. As argued by Varma (2002), social constructionist framework has renewed interest in cultural and historical understanding of psychological theories. Feminist and indigenous psychologies are outgrowth of such critical analysis of the existing body of research.

The post-modernism and social constructionism are, in this respect, much closer to the non-dualism of the knower and the known in Indian epistemological tradition (Radhakrishnan, 1953, p. 95). Self is both the knower and the known, and no observations can be independent of the nature of self. At the core of the self is *ego* which creates a dualism, a false notion of the independence of knower from the subject matter, that is independence of subjective experience and scientific reality. Indeed, self as ego is an accumulation of all memories of past experiences which provides the basis to interpret new experiences. Ego creates a centre and its motives and desires form the basis of building a knowledge base. All the knowledge so generated is nothing but construction (Krishnamurti, 1976). A true seeker of knowledge is expected to dissolve his/her ego and become detached to the object of observation. Psychological state of the knower is thus a crucial factor in the kind of knowledge generated.

To conclude, it may be stated that work in the domain of social psychology of knowledge (which includes both, the sociology of knowledge and social constructionism) has brought the role of culture in knowledge generation back to the centre stage. The concerns and debates these approaches have raised, demolished the myth of a universal psychology and made people aware of the West-centric construction of psychological knowledge. This debate has now become part of the intellectual discourse in developing countries. Diverse perspectives have been brought out to explain the present state of the affairs. For example, Egyptian political thinker, Said, settled in the USA, concluded in his book *Orientalism* that research in Asian countries reflects the presumptions of Western superiority and operate as a serve-serving projection of the researcher's conceptions (Said, 1978). On the other side, Indian anthropologist of science Vishwanathan (1995) states that India with its liberal traditions has been a testing ground for modern Western science for many of its defeated ideas. In a society which welcomes ideas and ideologies, and celebrates differences rather than destroying them, India provides a stage for the drama of science as a cultural force. In the following section, the journey of Western psychology on Indian soil is retraced to substantiate the argument that there is a symbiotic relationship between science and society. That psychology in India is a product of a developing society which is economically and technologically dependent on the West.

The Indian Scenario

To come back to the narrative of psychology in India, as mentioned earlier it began as a Western science in India. All academic institutions of that period were modelled on the British pattern and psychology was no exception[1]. Psychological research and teaching of that period reflected the background and mindset of Indian psychologists who predominantly hailed from renascent middle-class urban elite who were products of the British educational system. This newly emerging social class identified more with the British than with their own culture. Impressed by the superiority of Western sciences, Indian psychologists pursued the goals of contributing to universal body of knowledge about human behaviour. As the academic world looked down upon its own cultural heritage, indigenous knowledge was kept out of academic discourse. Even though many psychologists of that era were staunch nationalists, they maintained a neutral stance in their scientific work. They were interested in culture-free universal science, not in local issues. Thus, rarely a dialogue took place between scientists and social reformists. Psychology remained confined to testing Western theories on Indian samples and developing Indian adaptations of Western psychological tests. Psychology was decontextualized to maintain a universalistic stance, considering culture as an extraneous intrusion (Gergen et al., 1996). The psychology which developed in this social milieu was, with few exceptions, an alien discipline.

One reason why academic psychology took so long in arriving on the scene was probably because the colonial rulers did not see much utility of psychology in consolidating their empire. This, for example, was not true in the case of sociology and social anthropology, which had much to contribute to the smooth functioning of colonial administration in India (Dhanagare, 1985). Indian culture and society was totally unfamiliar to the colonial officials when they first arrived. The unique systems of caste, religion, tribal and rural communities, rituals, beliefs, and traditions were all baffling to an Englishman. These had no parallel in the experiences of the Western societies. Thus, in the absence of proper understanding of Indian social realities, the colonial administrators were facing many problems in their smooth functioning. There was much urgency and support for research on these topics. Neither Indian psychology nor Western psychological research held any such promise and were largely ignored. It is understandable that the British did not promote psychology in India in the same way as they did in the case of sociology and social anthropology.

In fact, Indian culture with its liberal and multiple traditions did not offer resistance to this new emerging science. In the West, Descartean philosophy had to face opposition from theology for a long time. Psychoanalysis had a very controversial entry into Western society; many of the books by Freud were initially banned. In Calcutta University, when Girindra Shekhar Bose took over the reins from Sengupta and vigorously promoted psychoanalysis, nobody raised an eyebrow. The three main streams of academic psychology in India—experimental psychology, psychoanalysis, and intelligence testing—were viewed as culture free, justifying uncritical borrowing from the West.

Girindra Shekhar Bose (1887–1953) became a professor and head of the department of psychology at the age of 23 and remained active for more than five decades. Interestingly, like Freud who was the first self-analysed psychoanalyst, Bose too was India's first 'self-styled' analyst who founded the *Indian Psychoanalytic Society*, after corresponding with Freud and Ernst Jones in early 1920s. The bustling stories of initial psychoanalytic activities in colonial India that we hear today are entirely to his credit. Bose's psychoanalytically oriented writings on Indian cultural psyche, particularly his doctoral thesis on the concept of repression, and interpretation of many religious texts, are examples of such efforts.

Alignment with Western positivism gave Indian psychologists an opportunity to make a fresh beginning. The emerging scientific discipline of psychology gave rise to some hope of generating radically different explanations of the prolonged colonial rule. There were exciting possibilities of making important discoveries about Indian people and society. Also, one could hope that the explanations of positive science would provide the much needed respectability to Indian cultural practices and rituals. At the personal level, it gave a new respectability to the upwardly mobile psychology professionals who mostly hailed from upper-class Western-educated elite. Although, as Nandy (1995) stated in the context of Girindra Shekhar Bose, there was an awareness that the sectoral and unidimensional approaches of academic psychology cannot yield in-depth analysis of the socio-psychological problems of Indian society; it could also not establish durable links with Indian traditions and belief systems. The importation of psychoanalysis as a science in colonial India provides an interesting account of how a handful of Indian intellectuals in the early twentieth-century Bengal used psychoanalysis to both critique the orthodox culture of Hindu society and subtly contest the Orientalist theories and representations of the Indian natives (Bhatia, 2002).

Nandy (1995) further stated, 'As a result, the usual encounter between an ancient culture with its distinctive culture of science and an exogenous science with its own distinctive culture fractured the self-definition not only of Bose but of many others involved in the similar enterprise' (p. 83). Caught between the two worlds, Indian psychologists always had a problem in balancing between a number of polarities—metaphysical versus empirical, clinical versus experimental, and intuitive versus objective. The Indian mind, even if trained to be a scientist, often finds it difficult to ruthlessly pursue the objective reality, something which comes perhaps naturally to a Westerner. Thus, conflicting elements are resolved into a suspension rather than a solution (Kakar, 1982b, p. 11). Indian psychologists compartmentalized their work in Western psychological tradition from other scholarly and personally satisfying creative pursuits. They simultaneously lived in two different worlds without any significant overlap.

The end of the British rule was no end to the Western influence on psychology in India. The first Prime Minister, Nehru, was a staunch believer in Western science for its potential to usher India into a modern state. For Nehru, laboratories and dams were the temples of modern India (Vishwanathan, 1998). It was at his initiative that Gardner Murphy came to India to study communal carnage of the partition days. To catch up with the West in terms of socio-economic development, great interest was shown in importing Western science and technology. Many foreign collaborations and academic exchange programmes were started. A large number of Indian scholars joined American and British universities for education in Western theories and methods. The Euro-American model became the basis for large scale expansion of higher education in India. Flush with their foreign degrees, Indian psychologists on return to their parent institutions earnestly pursued the work they were doing in the West. They were more responsive to the developments in the West than in the Indian society. As a result, Western theories and concepts constituted the core of research and teaching programme in most of the Indian universities.

It should not, therefore, be surprising that Indian psychologists did not take interests in contemporary reformist movement nor in India's struggle for freedom. There is hardly any notable work by Indian psychologists of that period on Gandhi and his non-violence. This is not just a coincidence. The ethos of scientific psychology was on value neutral, culture free, and ahistorical research. Indian psychologists, though many of them were staunch nationalists and actively participated in the freedom movement in their personal life, did not have methodology and motivation to make it their academic pursuit. Being ambivalent between remaining closer to the native 'self' or to the educated, enlightened white man, the educated Indians subverted the role of culture, self, and subjectivity in their practice of psychology. Most Indian psychologists chose to ignore Indian history, culture and practices, even denigrating the Indian value system and social customs in order to seek respectability in the Western academic world. These remnants of colonial rule have salutary effect on the way psychology has grown in the academia in the post-Independence era. Western knowledge became the yardstick of academic achievement and excellence in the academic world. This phenomenon was not confined to academic world only but visible on the application side also. Just after Independence the government started psychological bureaus in different states, starting from Patna and Allahabad, to provide counselling and vocational guidance services to the general public. These bureaus used all Western tests, or their Indian variants, for diagnostic purpose. The vocational guidance they provided was not found of much relevance in Indian cultural context and by the end of 50s, these bureaus became almost defunct. Similarly, colonial values and biases entirely mapped our understanding of the subjective world of the mentally ill. The two national institutes of mental health in Bangalore and Ranchi were modelled on the pattern of the Maudsley Mental Hospital of London and followed almost the same diagnostic and treatment procedures. These institutions could not become the rallying point for mental health services in India. Bulk of the population still resort to traditional healing centres spread all over the country. Psychology as a deterministic, mechanistic, individualistic, and logico-positivist enterprise limited the scope of it being relevant to comprehend Indian social reality.

The fact that psychologists in India lived in two worlds did not change much after Independence, but rather became more pronounced. In most universities, psychology departments were established by splitting the departments of philosophy. As a result, a large number of philosophy faculty moved to the newly formed psychology departments; many who opted for psychology were those who saw better career opportunities in the new departments. This movement from philosophy to psychology was so pervasive that by the end of 1960s a majority of chairmen in psychology departments had a philosophy background. In normal course, it could have been a strong philosophical knowledge base for psychology, making it richer in terms of indigenous concepts and theories. But this did not happen. In their enthusiasm to establish a new identity as scientists, these faculty members with a background in philosophy completely dissociated themselves from their parent discipline. They were more fascinated by the idea of value-free and culturally neutral experimental work. The areas they showed interest in were memory, psychophysics, perception, learning, pattern recognition, etc., which could be studied without bringing in the cultural context. These faculty members from philosophy had little training in research methodology. Their major quest, therefore, was to acquire methodological sophistication and mastery over statistical techniques. In the process they became ardent adherents of Western research methods. Thus, despite their firm moorings in ancient Indian psychology, psychology in India did not reap the fruits of this unique advantage. Indian psychologists were still coexisting in two different worlds. As professionals they were engaged in scientific research based on Western models but to satisfy their creative urges they would engage in other activities. This Indian experience was not an exception in this respect. In neighbouring Pakistan (Ansari, 1990) and Bangladesh (Hamida Begam, 1990), it was the same story, as in many other former colonies.

The subsequent ostracism that psychology faced in the academia worsened due to the inertia and lackadaisical stance of many psychologists toward attending to relevant social problems, and their rigidities in exploring new epistemologies and cross-fertilizations within and outside the discipline, as they chose mere replication of outdated and acontextual Western psychological researches. Sitting rather too comfortably in the pigeonholes of the University departments, which do not mirror sociocultural realities of common man in India, psychologists have increasingly chosen to remain insular and unnecessarily self-absorbed. Even during the times when social sciences were revamping and scrutinizing their colonial baggage, essentially during 70s and early 80s, psychology remained far from this self-reflexive and deconstructive enterprise that was in many ways deeply political in character and calling. As a result, both in terms of ideological and epistemological shifts, psychology in India has chosen to live behind veils (Kumar, 2006). In the face of public and government apathy, and in the absence of any real demand for their products, psychology continued growing in India without any sense of direction.

The Nehruvian model of socio-economic development which India followed, heavily relied on Western technology and know-how continued to marginalize the role of psychology (of social sciences in general) in development programmes. The community development programmes which were launched in the first Five-Year Plan in 1952 in a big way were in collaboration with the experts from American universities and institutes (Jain, 1986). Even to study the communal violence during the partition of India, Prime Minister Nehru requested the UNESCO to commission someone, instead of relying on Indian psychologists. Gardner Murphy came to India to study partition riots and published a book *In the Minds of Men* (1953) in which many Indian psychologists also contributed. Ramasubban (1977) in her critic on the sociology of Indian social sciences observed that the Green Revolution of early 70s proved the efficacy of imported technology in the upward march of rural economy. Wholesale and continuous import of technology was found by all subsequent governments, a convenient substitute for investment in social sciences to effect social transformation. In all government policies, investment in technology was at the cost of science, where technology was the mantra for development. In fact, as Nandy (1988) argued, the boundaries between science and technology blurred, so much so that, 'In the name of science and development one can today demand enormous sacrifices from, and inflict enormous sufferings on, the ordinary citizens' (p. 1). The traditional values and way of living were seen as an impediment to scientific temper.

Nandy (1989) has referred to this phenomenon as 'second colonization' (p. xi). This kind of colonialism, he argued, colonizes the mind as well as the body and 'helps generalize the concept of modern West from a geographical and temporal entity to a psychological category. The West is now everywhere, within the West and outside; in structures and in minds' (Nandy, 1989, p. xii). Nandy (1989) further argued the point that this second form of colonization is as dangerous as the first kind, because it is 'almost always unconscious and almost always ignored ... it creates a culture in which the ruled are constantly tempted to fight their rulers within the psychological limits set by the latter' (p. 3). Nandy's (1989) remark captures the state of Indian psychology in the postcolonial context: Indian psychology in the postcolonial period continues to operate within the boundaries and limits that were set forth by Euro-American psychology. The early colonial Indian psychologists who were trained in Euro-American psychology were highly successful in setting up a legacy of Euro-American psychology in Indian universities and academic departments (Bhatia, 2002). Gergen et al. (1996) noted that the presence of Euro-American psychology within Indian universities was so strong and influential that many Indian psychologists maintained a 'distance' and often looked down on their own psychological traditions with absolute 'suspicion' (p. 497). Indian intellectuals believe that science, technology, and the principles of Western secularism and modernity will provide some answers to mass poverty, unemployment, and the rise of religious fundamentalism and ethnic violence in India.

Indian psychologists have primarily attempted to replicate or validate popular Western theories and researches without much emphasis or rigour shown in picking up context-relevant methodology or clear theoretical ideological considerations which guide their research questions in the first instance. Much of the research conducted in academic departments and published in Indian journals was based on testing of Western theories and research. Even the idioms and metaphors used were Western. This pattern was also reflected in the themes and contents of national and regional conferences and rarely any stimulating ideas were thrown up in such forums. The mainstream researcher focussed on domains of social, cognitive, developmental, and experimental psychology. The peculiarity of this literature is that it speaks to no one, attempts to replicate without clear logic or method, eschews subjectivity or any engagement with researcher's position, and fails to acknowledge how results are a direct outcome of the process and values the researcher chooses to adopt (Kumar, 2006). Though research output was massive in terms of number, these researches rarely emanated from the societal furnace, nor did they provide mirror to understand Indian culture. Voices of dissent were raised from many quarters against the imitative nature of research in mid-70s. As Nandy (1974) observed, 'Indian psychology has become not merely imitative and subservient but also dull and replicative' (p. 5). D. Sinha states, 'Indian psychologists have followed almost in entirety the disciplinary fashion prevalent in the West with regard to choice of topics, methods of investigation, and models and theoretical frameworks used for explaining them' (D. Sinha, 1986, p. 110). He exhorted Indian psychologists to use indigenous theoretical frameworks and tools to deal with Indian social problems. Clearly, psychologists in late 70s and onwards were under pressure to be relevant to the country's social, economic, and political agenda. By this time psychology had proliferated not only in academic institutions but the demand of psychologists was growing in industry, education, and NGO sectors where the demands and expectations were of applied nature.

As Vishwanathan (1995) writes, the real challenge to the present model of science came from the grass-roots movements. The movements like Chipko, Save Himalaya, Narmada Bachao, Azadi Bachao were basically against the inherent inhuman and violent aspects of Western science. These were the mass agitations in 1980s and onwards to make science culturally sensitive, to bring it closer to the people. This was the time when Swadeshi movement was picking up to promote Indian products by opposing Western multinationals and their products. These social movements not only challenged the legitimacy of establishment of scientific institutions but also became producers of scientific knowledge in their own right. Many incisive writings on the philosophy of science and social-psychology of development were brought out by the people educated in the field. It seems that Western psychology is stagnating in the academic setting, psychology of indigenous variety is not only outgrowing the alien framework but also outgrowing the academic system.

Persistent criticism of mainstream Western psychology from within and outside led to two new developments in India in late 70s and 80s. These were cross-cultural psychology and indigenous psychology. Cross-cultural psychology started building up in the West to test the applicability of Western theories in the third-world countries. By the mid-1970s, cross-cultural psychology had become a 'thriving intellectual enterprise', with the creation of international organizations and new journals for publishing research related to cross-cultural scholarship (Berry et al., 1992; Triandis, 1980). An examination of the research published in those journals and books in the last 30 years indicates that cross-cultural psychology has evolved by firmly adhering to the principles and objectives of mainstream American psychology (Triandis, 1980). Berry et al. (1992) were explicit about the three specific goals for cross-cultural psychology. The first goal essentially aims at transporting hypotheses and findings generated in Western universities to new cultural settings and contexts to test their applicability to other groups of people. The second goal of cross-cultural psychology is to 'explore other cultures in order to discover psychological variations that are not present in one's own limited cultural experiences' (p. 3). The third goal is an attempt to 'assemble and integrate' the results of the first two goals into a broad-based psychology that will closely resemble a 'more nearly universal psychology ... that will be valid for a broad range of cultures' (p. 3). Gergen et al. (1996, pp. 500–01) stated that cross-cultural psychologists were able to recognize the 'cultural shortsightedness of Western psychology', but overall 'they have been unable to abandon mainstream scientism in general and remain loyal to empiricism and test Western theories with "culturally" (i.e. geographically) diverse data'. In recent years cross-cultural psychology itself is going through a crisis; it remained a methodological enterprise in which culture is relegated to secondary concern.

Indian psychologists who had started questioning the Euro-American orientation of academic psychology in India and were uncomfortable with the replicative nature of Indian studies found cross-cultural psychology an ideal shift in their endeavours. It was an opportunity, particularly for those who were trained in the West, to continue working on the Western models and to test their generality in Indian cultural and subcultural settings. Cross-cultural psychology, in fact, provided new legitimacy to their research activities. At the same time being one of the 'most advanced' among the developing countries, it was an opening for Indian psychologists to take up leadership role in cross-cultural movement. In the last two or three decades particularly, a number of Indian psychologists were involved in international collaborations to test and extend the generality of Western theories.

Another diversion taken by psychology in India can be termed as indigenization, the process of making the discipline sensitive to cultural nuances and socially relevant. This turn in academic psychology is consistent with what was happening in other social sciences in India in the 80s (see Dhanagare, 1993). Prominent Indian psychologists built up a case for indigenous psychology to make it more relevant to local and cultural practices (for a review, see D. Sinha, 1986). The Canadian psychologist, John Adair, saw indigenization as a gradual process, and in collaboration with his Indian colleagues, developed a scale to measure the degree of indigenization. Adair (1989) operationalized indigenization in terms of the following: (i) cultural sensitivity of research in designing a study and discussing its findings, (ii) citation from one's own culture, (iii) problem orientation, (iv) development of culture-based concepts, theories, and methods, (v) culturally anchored tests, and (vi) cross-cultural comparisons. Adair and colleagues concluded on the basis of content analysis of a sample of over 300 journal articles that there was progress in indigenization of psychology in India, albeit at a slow pace (Adair, Puhan and Vohra, 1993). It is important to note in this context that, as Adair and others clarify, their focus is on the indigenization of an 'imported discipline', and not on 'endogenous development' of psychology based on indigenous sources. However, many Indian psychologists have described such exogenous indigenization as cosmetic and superficial.

However, many serious efforts to build a culturally sensitive social psychological research in India are evident. Indian psychologists were critical of McClelland and Winter's (1969) highly Eurocentric work on achievement motivation that they conducted in India in the 1960s, derived with the variant experimental findings (for a review, see J.B.P. Sinha, 1984). J.B.P. Sinha also came up with alternate leadership style 'nurturant task leader' appropriate in Indian culture. Other important work in the organization setting was by Pareek (1970), Chakraborty (1987, 1995), and Sharma (1999, 1996). Pareek (1967) proposed an alternative model of motivational structure for poverty reduction and socio-economic development. Chakraborty and Sharma worked on developing managerial training modules based on yogic practices and the Gita. Sudhir Kakar is perhaps the first Indian psychoanalyst to have extensively written and deliberated so poignantly and thoughtfully on wide socio-psychological forays. His pioneering work on Hindu conceptions of personhood, family, and psychological and spiritual healing traditions has contributed immensely in deconstructing the universal claims of psychoanalysis (1982, 1991, 1996). Neki's (1973) *guru–chela* theory provides an alternative therapeutic model in clinical practices. D. Sinha (1983, 1986) and Sinha and Tripathi (1994) were concerned about making psychology relevant to socio-economic development of India. Saraswathi (1999, 1998), Bhargavi Davar (1999), and U. Vindhya (2003) have attempted to engage with questions of suffering; identity politics, and self-processes in situations of massive trauma; and the attendant existential concerns of women's lives. Most of this research has built on the mainstream (Western) psychology, while taking into consideration history, traditions, scriptures, and socio-political conditions.

It is, however, too early to conclude that psychology in India is weaning away from the Western influence. As J.B.P. Sinha (1996) observed, though there are few front runners who are treading new pathways, the big bulk is still of the replications of the Western studies. The academic socialization of Indian psychologists and disciplinary ethos restricts the range of their inquiry. As Holzner (1968) stated, the epistemic communities working in the academic setting build their own language, hierarchy, traditions, ethics, and mode of thinking, and resist any external pressure to change. These communities bound by power relationships have created social systems to ensure conformity by controlling reward system and information channels. In India, these epistematic communities indoctrinated in Western psychology remained self-serving, mutually supportive within the confines of their disciplinary boundaries. The predominantly urban middle-class background of the Indian psychologists (Dalal, 1990; Pareek, Dixit, and Saruparla, 1979) are low on risk taking and high on conforming to the prevalent academic culture. Stuck in the grooves of replicative research and antiquated teaching programmes, academic departments lost their capacity to resonate with the problems and challenges of a developing society.

The opening up of the Indian economy and strong winds of globalization has further complicated the scenario. The changes in political culture and social values have rendered the existing paradigm of science completely irrelevant. At times one gets an impression that incessant criticism and scrutiny of Western research and call for indigenization of psychology is having desired impact. But like Swadeshi movement which is swarmed by the market forces, the indigenization of psychology is also getting caught in the quagmire of contrasting visions of development. At one end is the burgeoning middle class cherishing an American dream of development of science cities, supermarkets, computers, fast food, etc. The impressive growth of Indian economy can, in a way, attribute to the adoption of Western technology by mastering it and using it to compete with the industrialized world. The information revolution has changed the complexion of the world. In global world, children in Indian schools are studying books written in the West, printed in Singapore and distributed by multinational chains. On the other end, are tribals and poor for whom modernity and science have become ways of oppression.

Their voices are muffled by the razzle-dazzle of booming economy. Both popular media and civil societies are swarmed by market culture and entrepreneurial ethos. There are many exciting innovations and experiments going on in the society and we need different paradigms to make sense of them. We need a psychology which can bridge the gap between science and society in transition.

The hierarchical and seniority conscious Indian psychologists subscribed conventional approach to research and teaching. These are often the seniors who set the agenda of research and course curriculum which is unmindfully pursued by the junior faculty and research scholars. In a system where merit and work are rarely considerations in promotion, research has low priority in universities and institutions. Political and caste considerations which have plagued the Indian society also cast its shadow in the academic world. Unsure of their survival without flaunting their extra-academic affiliations the academic faculty rarely takes research as a serious pursuit. This is the backdrop in which a lackadaisical attitude toward professional work becomes the general ethos. This explains why there are few examples of thematic long-term research projects carried out by Indian psychologists. There is unthoughtful usage of Western textbooks or their poor Indian imitations at undergraduate as well as postgraduate level with little efforts to update course contents. Often, there is no concern about theoretical underpinnings of psychological tests so much so that tests based on contrasting constructs are uncritically used in the same context.

In the last 20 years, a few Euro-American and third-world psychologists have seriously examined the legitimacy of exporting Euro-American psychology as a universal science to non-Western societies (Blackler, 1983; Enriquez, 1993; Kim and Berry, 1993; Moghaddam, 1987; Owusu-Bempah and Howitt, 2000). However, most Indian and other non-Western psychologists continue to work within the confines of Euro-American psychology, and therefore the emergence of alternative indigenous psychologies on a global scale has either been nonexistent or very gradual.

Emergence of Indian Psychology

A different kind of indigenization which focuses on the contemporary relevance of cultural heritage and native theories is termed as 'Indian Psychology'. J.B.P. Sinha (2002) has referred to this kind of indigenization as 'purist trend' which is based on a systematic analysis of the culture-bound concepts and categories. Such indigenization has primarily relied on the rich storehouse of knowledge found in Indian scriptures and philosophical texts of last two or three millennia. The plurality of Indian tradition and ethos of accommodating diverse thought systems provide a rich gold mine for creatively building a new psychology. It may be relevant to state here that historically a distinction is made between *Indian psychology* and *psychology in India* which is used to denote practice of psychology in general in the country. This is to differentiate Indian psychological viewpoints (culturally rooted/indigenous viewpoints) from the twentieth-century Western psychology in India.

Indian psychology has developed around the existential quest to overcome human suffering and in the process raised the person to higher levels of awareness and achievement. Thus, Indian psychology endeavours not only to provide an understanding of the nature of a person, the causes and consequences of his/her conduct, but also to explore the methods and means of transforming the person in pursuit of perfection in being, certainty in knowing, and happiness in feeling. Indian psychology focuses on the inner-self which is accessible through subjective methods of self-verification. The beginning of Indian psychology can be traced in the writings of many eminent thinkers, like Vivekananda and Sri Aurobindo in the early part of the last century. The monumental work of Jadunath Sinha (1934/1958, 1961) on Indian psychology can be considered as a landmark in formally establishing it as an independent discipline. The books of Ramachandra Rao (*Development of Psychological Thought in India*, 1962) and Ragunath Safaya (*Indian Psychology*, 1975) gave it further impetus in the early years. These efforts to rejuvenate psychology in the ancient texts intensified in the 80s and 90s. Some notable publications of this period are by Chakraborty (1995), Paranjpe (1998, 1984), Ramakrishna Rao (2005, 2002, 1988), and Saraswathi (1999). There is a rich and growing body of research in this area and many excellent reviews are available. This stream has built not only on the interpretation of traditional concepts and theories in contemporary idiom, but also on their integration within a broader, global perspective. It is argued that psychological knowledge from the Indian spiritual tradition needs to be integrated in the teaching programmes. According to Cornelissen, the core of its curriculum could be Indian theories of self and consciousness.

Four factors have contributed to this change of attitudes and perceptions of Indian psychology. One is the failure of Western psychology to deal with their own societal problems. It has increasingly been realized that positivistic psychology only provides a fragmented and superficial understanding of human feelings and behaviour. The growing problems of social and family violence, mental health, moral decay, etc., have brought out the gross limitations of mainstream Western psychology. Humanistic and transpersonal movements in the 60s have been the protest movements against brute empiricism in psychological research. A need was felt to bring back spirituality and religiosity in psychological research, which were banished from psychology for almost a 150 years (see special issue of the *American Psychologist*, January 2004). All these contemporary developments are in response to the acutely felt limitations of psychology developed within the framework of modern science, which led to new ways of thinking in terms of feminism, social constructionism, postmodernism, and the like which are much closer to Eastern philosophies. The movement toward positive psychology (Snyder and Lopez, 2002) also has many ingredients of Indian psychology.

Two, is the growing popularity of yoga and other spiritual systems of India in the West. In the past few decades, more and more persons with spiritual training and experiences from India have been visiting other countries and have acquired large following. They have been responsible for disseminating the Indian spiritual tradition. Among them, Sri Aurobindo, Maharshi Mahesh, and Swami Rama are some prominent gurus who have been able to draw the attention of academic psychologists. Sri Aurobindo's *Integral Yoga* and *Integral Psychology* attracted worldwide attention. Mahesh Yogi's transcendental meditation went through rigorous experimental testing at Harvard and many other universities. Swami Rama offered himself to extensive medical testing at the Menninger Foundation Laboratory, New York, where he demonstrated many yogic feats. These Indian masters were able to demonstrate convincingly the power of mind over body and have contributed significantly toward evoking interest in the Indian psychological perspectives. Publications of

Sri Aurobindo Ashram, Puducherry, and the Himalayan International Institute for Yoga Sciences, Philosophy, and Religion in Honesdale, Pennsylvania, founded by Swami Rama, are valuable for their significant contributions in expounding the psychological insights of *Vedanta*, *Yoga*, *Samkhya*, and other Indian systems. These and many other accomplished spiritual masters of the Indian tradition have played important role in popularizing Indian psychology in the world (Paranjpe, 2006).

Three, is the secular nature of Indian psychology. It is a gradual acknowledgement that Indian psychology of consciousness has much to offer in terms of self-growth rather than as religious traditions. Interest in the study of altered state phenomena since 1960s and the founding of transpersonal psychology as a sub-discipline, encouraged psychologists involved in them to examine the indigenous perspectives available in many religious traditions of the East. It was recognized clearly that modern psychology has nothing to offer regarding the spiritual/transcendental dimension of human nature either to understand others or for personal growth (Tart, 1975). Unfortunately, many academic psychologists in India have not appreciated this fact and consider Indian psychology as part of the revivalistic movement.

Four, with India emerging as a major economic power in the world, there is a renewed interest in Indian values, philosophies, and practices, as well as in the strength and resilience of Indian society. The very Indian culture and philosophy which was debunked for India's poverty and backwardness by many Western Indologists (Max Muller, and others) is now seen behind India's success stories. Indian research is now taken more seriously by Western psychologists, and as a consequence (ironically), by Indian psychologists themselves.

In more recent times, efforts to build Indian psychology as a vibrant discipline have intensified. Several conferences (Delhi, 2007; Kollam, 2002; Puducherry, 2001, 2002, 2004; Vishakhapatnam, 2004) in recent times have given impetus to this movement of Indian psychology. A number of publications on Indian psychology, such as Kuppuswami's *Elements of Ancient Indian Psychology* (1985), Indra Sen's *Integral Psychology* (1986), Misra and Mohanty's *Perspectives on Indigenous Psychology* (2002) have the potential of serving as textbooks and more recently, Joshi and Cornelissen's edited volume, *Consciousness, Indian*

Psychology and Yoga (2004); K.R. Rao and Marwaha's *Towards a Spiritual Psychology* (2005); K.R. Rao, Paranjpe, and Dalal's *Handbook of Indian Psychology* (2008), and Cornelissen, Misra, and Verma's *Foundations of Indian Psychology* (2011), and Rao and Paranjpe's *Psychology in the Indian Tradition* (2015).

Psychology in the New Millennium

Clearly, by the turn of this new millennium, the academic scenario is changing in India. Psychologists in India are increasingly getting aware of the wide gap between their academic pursuits and the real-life problems of people. The replicative nature of research endeavours, antiquated and obsolete teaching programmes, and lack of applied orientation have devoid the discipline of any professional momentum. Indian psychologists want to break free from the theoretical and methodological constraints of the discipline to grapple with the real issues of development and to act as social catalysts in the change process. Indian psychologists are also aware that if they fail to take up the challenge, they are likely to be completely marginalized.

The concern over the dominance of American psychology and attempts to develop psychology appropriate to indigenous cultures and societies is common not only to the third-world countries but also to the second-world countries of Europe (Moghaddam, 1987). The need for developing indigenous perspectives of one's culture has been felt by psychologists in many countries in all the continents. Thus, it is not a culture-specific phenomenon, limited to a few Asian societies. Indian psychology is indigenous psychology in that it is a psychology derived from indigenous thought systems and therefore is clearly best suited to address India's specific psychological issues and problems. It is, however, more than indigenous psychology for the reason that it offers psychological models and theories appropriate to address problems of social conflicts, violence, and mental health in other societies. The scientific community is better prepared now than in the past to accept a psychology rooted in native wisdom and philosophical traditions.

However, a debate is still raging within the scientific community about retaining Western scientific paradigm of psychological research in India. The proliferation of academic institutions modelled on implicit supremacy of Western science and its failure in addressing India's complex problems of socio-economic development has intensified this debate in recent times. We are still trying to comprehend what happens to a modern science in the firmament of an ancient civilization. A vast majority of Indian psychologists, though critical of the replicative and imitative nature of their research, are not prepared to 'go back to ancient scriptures and texts' for spiritual and intellectual enlightenment and apply its prescriptions to deal with the problems with national concern. To them Indian psychology is too esoteric and mystical to deal with the complex problems of modern society. Many see in Indian psychology an agenda of 'Hindutva' and thus it sounds like a revivalist game plan of the RSS and the BJP. Psychologists who are concerned about secular and scientific stature of the discipline are guarded in their response to Indian psychology. They wish to remain part of the mainstream psychology.

The point is that there is a need to broaden the framework within which a positive, constructive dialogue about an alternative science of psychology can take place. Rather than debunking and denouncing imitative research conducted in colonial and postcolonial India, it will be more fruitful to comprehend socio-political compulsions which shaped the discipline. A comprehensive, empathetic appreciation of the present state of affairs demand that rather than viewing the situation from within narrow disciplinary boundaries, we step out and look at the discipline from outside. As Vishwanathan (1998) argued, the liberal and plural Indian society has provided a unique opportunity to understand how an alien science was internalized and reinvented in the postcolonial India. In the rapidly changing world scenario, Indian urban elite is confronted with the monumental civilizational integration of various aspects of Westernization within the broad syncretic framework of Hinduism. In the progress of psychology in India any wholesale rejection of Western knowledge will be counterproductive (Pandey, 1988).

The emerging discipline of psychology in India should be able to accommodate both Western scientific knowledge and ancient Indian wisdom. What we need is psychology as a science of the Indian people. It envisions a discipline whose boundaries are permeable and dynamically defined. A discipline with multiple psychologies which meets the aspirations of burgeoning middle class with the American dream, and also, those of the Dalits and the downtrodden, a psychology leading to emancipation. It should pave the way to create multiple psychologies with different beliefs, values, and visions. In such disciplinary ethos, perception and construction of social reality becomes a joint responsibility of scientists and common man. It is a vision of a vibrant and responsive science that must thrive on differences in perspectives and understanding of realities.

Many in the academics have raised the concern that psychology as a scientific discipline is losing its lustre and is on decline. The question which is asked is, 'How to rejuvenate psychology in India?' In its long journey as a Western science, psychology has lost its steam and lustre, and has become stale and sterile. The answer lies in reinventing psychology from a recipient science to a proficient forum for dialogue on issues vital to Indian society, the society, and to the global world. With its rich cultural heritage and liberal traditions, the discipline has an unenviable advantage of taking a leap in the direction of human growth and inner development. In many ways psychology in India is all set to turn a new leaf in the new millennium.

Note

1. Adas (1989) mapped out in comprehensive detail how eighteenth- and nineteenth-century European countries used the power of technology and science to justify the 'civilizing mission' in non-Western colonies. To justify colonization, they asserted the intellectual supremacy of the West by attributing traits of rationality, modernity, and objectivity to the Western culture.

6

A Four-Decade Long Journey Back to the Basics

On September 8, 2015, I completed my four-decade long service as a psychology faculty at the Allahabad University. Superannuation from the same university job is thus an occasion to take stock of my academic journey and look forward to the next phase of my work-life. I will be moving to my native place of Udaipur and engage in writing in public fora on a fulltime basis. Before leaving Allahabad, I owe, to my colleagues, students, and well-wishers, a narrative account of my foray into academic psychology and personal report card.

Doing master's in psychology was my own decision against the wishes of my family. I wanted to be a freelance fiction writer and wanted to make it my career. I wanted to write about resilience, thriving on crises, and the undying human spirit. Those days I was a vociferous reader of Hindi fiction and was writing short stories. I was getting convinced that a systematic study of psychology would prepare me to be a fiction writer of some worth. As a fiction writer I could sit in a remote corner and write, away from the public glare. I was too conscious of my physical disability and my awkward walking on crutches. As a fiction writer, I could have easily avoided public appearance. At the same time I was ambitious and wanted to pursue my career with vigour and greater independence.

I had already completed my master's in mathematics and thought that it was high time to study psychology in some other town. My family could not understand how I would be able to survive on my own. To me, however, doing a master's degree in psychology seemed promising for opening new avenues in lives. There was no department of psychology in the University of Udaipur at that time and my options of moving out were rather limited. Two nearest towns where I could have studied psychology were Ahmedabad and Jodhpur. I went and met Prof Bhopatkar in Ahmedabad who advised that I should study economics instead of psychology. In the University of Jodhpur, my maternal uncle was a faculty in the department of business administration. Prof M.C. Joshi of the Banaras Hindu University had just joined the University of Jodhpur as a professor and head of the department of psychology. Given his encouragement and advice, I gladly decided to pursue my master's degree in psychology at the University of Jodhpur. I moved to Jodhpur, and lived on the campus in Jaswant hostel. The son of a hostel employee helped me commute to the *Department of Psychology* every day.

I was the only one in my group who already had one master's degree but no background in psychology. My peers were studying psychology at a higher level; I was just picking up basic psychological facts and concepts. Woodworth and Schlosberg's (1970 edition) book was the main textbook in the course on *Experimental Psychology*. I had difficulty in comprehending the terms stimulus (S) and response (R), as they were often defined in relation to each other. The S–R paradigm was later supplemented by the S–O–R paradigm in which O stood for organism, which was like a black box and one could only conjecture whatever was happening inside it. Learning theories in psychology courses were based on this paradigm; so were other courses on personality, social testing, and clinical psychology. By the end of my first year of postgraduate study, my dream of pursuing a literary career by studying psychology was rather shattered! Nevertheless, a new dream of becoming an academic psychologist caught my imagination.

After completing the master's, thus, the logical pursuit was to have a doctoral degree in psychology. There were three universities in Rajasthan but nowhere was a slot open with psychology professors to take more doctoral students. Out of desperation, I wrote to other centres—the Institute of Education, Baroda, where the legendary Prof M.N. Buch was working, the Birla Institute of Technology at Pilani, and the Indian Institute of Technology, Kanpur (IIT-K). From all the three institutes, I got very encouraging response. In fact, one day Prof M.C. Joshi came to my hostel room in Jodhpur and asked me to send my application to IIT-K. He informed me that a professor from Jodhpur was going there and he would take my application. Eventually, in January 1975, I joined IIT-K as a doctoral student.

Two young America-trained psychologists, namely, Ramadhar Singh and Janak Pandey had recently joined IIT-K as assistant professors and they started a doctoral programme in psychology. Three of the four psychology faculty in the department were trained in the US, and their model of doctoral programme was patterned after that of the American schools. I was one of the three students admitted to the first group of doctoral students. The enthusiasm of the faculty and the general ethos of IIT-K played a major role in our academic and professional grooming. After the first semester, we three students were appointed as teaching assistants and were assigned tutorial classes of the engineering students. More doctoral students joined in the next semester and the psychology group became sizeable. We completed nine semester courses and qualified a comprehensive examination before becoming a doctoral candidate.

I selected Assistant Prof Ramadhar Singh, who had done his PhD with Prof Donn Byrne, an internationally famous psychologist for his research in attitude similarity–interpersonal attraction. Prof Byrne and his colleague Prof Robert A. Baron brought out a textbook on social psychology which became a popular reading in English-speaking countries. When Byrne came to know about Meenakshi Gupta and me joining with Prof Singh for a PhD degree, he sent us copies of that textbook and we were joyous. Both of us in fact, did not work on Prof Byrne's theory. Prof Singh, by that time, was getting more interested in Prof Norman H. Anderson's Information Integration Theory and I also took up my doctoral work in that area.

Prof Anderson also had a master's degree in mathematics and then a doctoral degree in psychology. He was basically interested in examining how our mind integrates different pieces of information and takes decisions, using integration rules of adding, subtracting, multiplying, and dividing. Prof Anderson developed experimental methods and used analysis of variance (ANOVA) as a statistical tool to unravel these mathematical rules. Prof Anderson's theory works with chunks of information, whereas Prof Byrne's theory includes the affective aspect. In those days there was intense debate about how the effective and cognitive loadings of information could be independently processed in our decision-making, and whether it was possible? There were articles in journals which we had read and discussed in our group. Given my mathematical background, I was more impressed by the scientific rigour and mathematical formulation of Anderson's work. Following his methodology, I designed my experiments in which participants were asked to evaluate different job offers which varied on four factors—pay, nature of work, job security, and achievement. Each information was varied at two levels and all combinations of these factors were taken to have 16 job descriptions, adding to it the job descriptions based on two pieces of job information only. IIT-K students, who served as participants in my experiments, rated these hypothetical job offers for their attractiveness. The objective was to unravel the arithmetic rule which our mind uses to integrate different pieces of information. I prepared the research proposal on which I got encouraging feedback from Prof Anderson. Prof Singh was very supportive and I immersed in research wholeheartedly.

I mostly worked in the psychology lab which was on the ground floor. I rarely went to HSS department for classes, which was on the sixth floor of the building. Often the lift was out of order, and the faculty would come down to take classes in the lab, to save me from the hassle of climbing stairs on crutches. As students, we had the opportunity of meeting a stream of distinguished visitors from all over the country and sometimes from outside the country. Often we were also invited to join the dinner hosted by Prof Pandey and Prof Singh at their houses and got a chance to know these visitors personally.

A few months before I completed my thesis, Prof Pandey asked me one day if I would consider applying for a faculty position at the University of Allahabad. I had not seriously thought about a job till that time, but gave my tentative consent. I had met Prof Sinha and Dr Tripathi who had visited IIT-K two–three times. I had done some computer analysis for Prof Sinha and so, had interacted with him on a few occasions. Many PhD students from the Allahabad psychology department had visited IIT-K, so I was familiar with the department at Allahabad University. Within a month I got an interview call and went to Allahabad to appear before the selection committee. I was taken in as a lecturer and was asked to join at the earliest. I talked to Prof Pandey, who knew about it and suggested me to seek an extension of the joining date to complete my thesis work.

The prospect of joining at Allahabad created an urgency of completing the thesis work. I was not inclined to join at Allahabad without submitting my thesis. I was halfway in my data collection and then I still had to do the analysis and the report writing. The institute gave me a small grant to expedite the data-collection work. In the day time, I would collect data on two or three students, and would go to the computer centre to analyse that data in the evening. I was analysing the data of each student separately to find the arithmetic rule he or she was using. Working till late at night and feeling hungry, me and my friends would go to *chungi* (city checkpost) to eat at the roadside *dhaba* (eatery) and return well past midnight. In the early morning, while on his morning walk, Prof Singh would often drop by to discuss the computer analysis which I had done the previous evening. Sitting in the lab, when not collecting data, I concentrated on writing my already completed two experiments.

The deadline of my joining the job at Allahabad was approaching. I had already got two extensions and there was no possibility of getting third. I had to join on April 24. I reached Allahabad on the evening of April 23 with my friend Mrinal and we stayed with his elder sister. In the morning we came to the department. The university was disturbed due to student agitation and the see-saw fight was going on between the police and the students at the Union Gate when I reached the campus. I was led inside from the other gate. The department was deserted but Prof Tripathi was there knowing that I was coming to join. He asked the office to prepare my joining report and I completed the official paperwork. Prof Pandey had joined there a few weeks earlier as professor. This development came as a surprise to me.

I came to the department for another two days but the university was still disturbed. On the third day the Vice Chancellor closed the university for summer vacations and I returned back to IIT to complete my PhD in the summer months.

Before joining at Allahabad in April, I had finished a bulk of the writing work and had given it to Prof Singh for his approval. On my return from Allahabad after three days, I realized that he did not approve of it and it had to be redone all over again. Every day in the morning I would do my homework and then go to Prof Singh's house where he would work with me till late afternoon. Often I had my lunch at his place. I would fair out and finalize the write up by evening, and would give it for typing. This routine continued for almost two months and finally the thesis was over. It was the first thesis in our group and everyone really put in their efforts in seeing it through.

In the middle of July, my father came from Udaipur and we drove to Allahabad with the luggage in my three-wheeler. We were in Allahabad by evening and put up in a hotel near the railway station. After much searching, we eventually found a place to live in the Kareli scheme, which was about 10 km from the university. Kayyum, who intended to enrol with Prof Pandey for PhD, was to come here from IIT and we were to stay together in that house.

The department was given the status of Centre for Special Assistance by the UGC and also a project on social psychology of education, under which many new faculty and other research positions were awarded to the department. About 8–10 of us joined as young faculty in the department, besides others. Ten teachers from other universities joined the department for their doctoral degree, apart from the 25 or so other PhD students. This influx changed the complexion of the department. With so much youthful energy, there was a spurt of research and other activities in the department. There was a consensus to start doctoral courses in the department based on IIT pattern. Prof Pandey began a course on social psychology and I on research methodology, which were joined by all PhD students, including teacher fellows and new faculty. It was a challenge for me to teach a class of 40 participants, half of them elder to me in age. The course was primarily on analysis of variance, in which Prof Singh also came to teach for a week. I really worked hard in that course and had the satisfaction that it went off well.

That was the period when we had many Fulbright scholars in the department. They also joined in offering doctoral courses. Prof Tripathi and Prof Bob Caplan offered a course on survey research methods, Prof Berman and his wife Jinni came from Nebraska University and offered a course on motivation. These courses and research activities were changing the complexion of the department.

Toward the end of 1978, I went to IIT for my PhD defence. Prof Puhan came as an external examiner from Bhubaneshwar. I think I defended my work well, as I gathered from the feedback of others in the seminar hall. On my return to Allahabad, I gave a talk on my doctoral work in the department. It was also attended by the faculty members from the Mehta Research Institute, mostly IITians. They came up with a plan of collaborative research in the area of information integration theory. But my heart was no more in that kind of research. To me it was just verbal manipulation and obtained arithmetic rules which were methodological artefacts. I wanted to change my research area but was not getting any direction. At that time, a paper written by Prof Singh got published (in which I was also a co-author) entitled 'Cultural differences in the attribution of performance'. The work was based on Anderson's model and the term 'attribution' was a misnomer. But the word caught my imagination and I started reading more on attribution research. I was a bit familiar with the work of Heider, Kelley, Jones, and Weiner, who were pioneers in the field of attribution research. So then, I started a project with two other colleagues, to study the children of ex-criminal tribes living in a government hostel in Allahabad. Some tribes were historically engaged in criminal activities and were labelled as criminal tribes by the colonial government. These tribes were denotified in free India but were popularly known as ex-criminal. The children of these tribes were weaned away from their families and placed in fully-funded government hostels. By the time these children reached early adolescence, they become aware why they were separated from the family. Their resentment manifested in destructive behaviour in the hostel and school. We studied attribution of blame in these children across developmental stages. In our overenthusiasm, we sent the paper both to the *Journal of Social Psychology* and to the *International Journal of Psychology*. Contrary to our expectations, the paper was immediately accepted by both the journals. We were jubilant but later realized that sending a paper to two journals simultaneously was unethical. We apologized to the editor of *International Journal of Psychology* and withdrew our paper from that journal.

The other significant research piece I did during that period was a study of the validity of rating scales as measurement tools. I had used a 31-point rating scale in my PhD work which the participants used comfortably with some practice in making judgements in experimental situations. Many in the department questioned the validity of such a big scale. I planned a study in which 3, 7, 11, 15, and 31-point scales were given to different groups of participants. Participants were given two tasks—one was to study the faces in which the smile line varied from sad to happy (systematically changed from convex to concave), and in the other task, a list of jobs, varying in prestige value was studied. Participants rated these stimuli for happiness and status value, using different rating scales. I also made post-experimental inquiry to know the strategies which the subjects employed while using the rating scales having different scale points. The findings showed that line graphs for different scales were parallel and the correlations across different rating scales were high. Post-experimental inquiry revealed that as strategy the participants divided the scale in a low and high side and kept dividing it further to choose the appropriate rating point to mark their judgements. I based my paper on the range- frequency theory of Prof Allan Parducci. I sent the paper to Prof Parducci for his feedback. He sent me a four-page long comment, and redrew my graphs to make better sense of them. The paper got published in the *Journal of General Psychology*. I had the satisfaction that I could validate the 31-point rating scale which I had used in my thesis work.

There were always visitors in the department from abroad and within the country. There were lectures, seminars, and meetings, which kept the new faculty quite busy. Every time a new visitor arrived, Prof Sinha would call all of us for a meeting, where we were supposed to tell the visitor about our research. Such meetings used to be quite taxing but these pushed us to keep working and improving with the feedback received.

One day Prof Pandey asked me to apply for the Fulbright Fellowship. Prof Tripathi had availed it the previous year and that year Prof Naidu had gone to Michigan as a Fulbright Fellow. I applied and was awarded the fellowship. I decided to work at the University of California, Los Angeles (UCLA), with Prof Bernard Weiner. Prof Weiner's work in the area of causal attribution was well known and I considered myself fortunate for this opportunity. I had six months' time for joining there and collected data for two studies testing Weiner's attribution theory. I took the data with me to UCLA.

Los Angeles is the second largest city in the USA, and I had to struggle initially to find a place to live and arrange a vehicle to commute. UCLA was one of the top ten universities in the US and the psychology department was a massive 11-floor building, with three floors at sub-ground level. It had a faculty of 80, taking all areas of psychology together. I found Prof Weiner very friendly, cordial, and concerned. Everyone called him Bernie. I joined his doctoral class and became part of his discussion group. He had his class only once a week for four hours. At the end of the class, we all would sit together and eat. There used to be intense discussion in which everyone would participate, many questioning Bernie's attribution theory, and he would patiently reply. I realized how a good teacher could inspire and motivate his students, and mentor them. I became personally close to Prof Weiner, Prof Kelley, Prof Bert Raven, and other faculty members and was invited to their homes for dinner.

I analysed the data which I had collected in India and showed the results to Bernie. The results were not supportive of his theory and thus Bernie asked me to reanalyse the data in a different way. I did that but the results were again at odds with his theory. He kept insisting that there must have been something wrong with my research design that he could not elaborate. I realized how protective one might be of one's theory or attitude. My experiences with Prof Kelley were no different either. While attending classes by Prof Kelly, we were invited to come up with a critique of his theory of interpersonal relations. When students started enumerating flaws in his theory, Prof Kelley first heard everyone patiently, then began justifying his position, and finally lost his cool. In the subsequent class, his annoyance was even more perceptible, and he went to the extent of accusing us of being too unreasonable. He stunned us by his anger. But he realized what he did and a couple of days later apologized to the class for losing his temper. Apart from this stray incident, I was struck by Prof Kelley's humility; he did not carry an aura and air, as seemingly big professors in India do. In the very same year, Prof Kelly was adjudged the most eminent scholar of social psychology by the American Psychological Association.

I did one research project with Bernie on methodological issues which he sent to the *Journal of Personality and Social Psychology*. The paper got good reviews but the manuscript was not accepted for publication. I was a bit surprised that Bernie's paper could be rejected by the editors, but realized what professionalism means to American psychologists. At the same time I was getting disillusioned with sophisticated research designs, which may facilitate publication in good journals but might not address substantive practical issues. With four attribution categories of ability, effort, task difficulty, and luck, Bernie had created the whole edifice of his Motivational Theory of Achievement Motivation, which I found of little practical concern. Attribution research in that sense was no different from information integration research with which I was already disillusioned.

I noticed that the faculty and students at UCLA were more interested in knowing what kind of psychology we have in India. My answer that it was very much the same as in the West, often turned them off. I started reading more about psychology in India. I sat in the library for long hours, studied history of psychology in India, and prepared extensive notes. I was invited by two universities to speak on psychology in India, and discussion with the faculty charged my interest in this area. It so happened that for some time a Korean psychologist Shin-Ho-Ann, a Fulbright scholar, stayed in my office for a few weeks. He was working on the Buddhist concept of *Karuna* (pathos) and was looking at it from a cultural perspective. Talking to him brought significant changes in my thinking. I was convinced that we needed to do research on Indian concepts and theories. I was also much influenced by the work of Shelley Taylor, who was a research professor and her office was three rooms away from mine. Her work in the area of coping with tragic life events made a decisive shift in my research interest. We talked a few times about her work but I was shy to take further initiative about research collaboration.

My time of leaving UCLA was coming closer. One day, Prof Bert Raven, Chairman of the Psychology Department, took me to the Faculty Club. Over tea he tried to convince me that I should stay back; he said he could arrange for me some fellowship or project position. He argued that the scholars who came under the Fulbright programme at a young age rarely went back. I had made up my mind to return back to India as I was convinced that my work would be more meaningful in my own country.

Before leaving LA, I consulted some orthopaedic doctors at the famous Santa Monica Hospital. The orthopaedic doctor there did a thorough check up and suggested me to go for corrective spinal surgery as early as possible. That surgery was not feasible in the US in that trip, so I decided to consult doctors in India on return.

Before returning back to India, I went to the Institute for Survey Research (ISR), Ann Arbor, Michigan, the famous institute established by Kurt Levin. I stayed there for two months. Prof Bob Caplan who was in our department for eight months, was a faculty there. That was summer time and the institute was almost deserted. I met a few stalwarts, like Prof Richard Nisbett, Prof Michael Birbaum, Prof Gregary Markus, and others. I was keen to meet Prof Kamille Wortman who was a faculty there and had done extensive work in the area of coping with undesirable life events. She was on maternity leave but we talked on the phone and she made her publications available to me. I had been reading since quite some time about coping with tragic life events and was convinced that on return that would be my main area of research.

By the end of 1983, I was back in Allahabad and tried to get back in my research and teaching rhythm. In the beginning of next year, I got my promotion as a Reader in the department. During that period, I went twice to Mumbai to consult doctors and it became clear that I had to go through a major surgery for spinal deformity. There was a good deal of uncertainty about my physical condition after the surgery. I was not sure whether I would be able to resume work at Allahabad or not. I took six months medical leave from the university and left Allahabad for my hometown, Udaipur. While in Udaipur, someone informed me that the interviews for the post of associate professor in psychology were to be held in the university. Hurriedly, I prepared my biodata and went for the interview. In the interview, the Vice Chancellor asked, why do you want to come to Udaipur leaving Allahabad University? I pointed out that from his office window my house was just 2 km away. I was selected and a temporary associate professor in the department was demoted. I requested few months' time for joining the job.

The spinal surgery was performed at the Bombay Hospital by an eminent surgeon, Dr Dholakiya. His team of surgeons opened my vertebra and inserted two steel rods, each of 16 inches, to correct the spinal deformity, in a 7–8 hour-long surgery. These rods were to stay life-long to support my vertebra. My parents and I stayed in the hospital for one month. The surgery was successful but it took me another six months to recuperate. I had to learn from scratch to walk with crutches again. On the last working day before summer vacations, I joined the Sukhadia University at Udaipur; and got another two months' time to recover.

From mid-July I started going to the university regularly. Compared to Allahabad, it was a small department of six faculty members in Udaipur, with Prof G.C. Rai as the Head. There was hardly any research activity in the department, and the courses were taught from age-old textbooks. There were five or six students in MA first year and only two in the final year, and three or four research students. For me, it was a major come down from the active, vibrant academic life of Allahabad. I had not yet fully recovered from the surgery but tried initiating some collaborative research programme to ground myself there. It did not make much headway. I was increasingly getting frustrated with my academic life in Udaipur. I did not feel like doing a stale routine teaching job and decided to return back to Allahabad. I wrote to Prof R.C. Tripathi and to the Vice Chancellor that if I would get university accomodation in Allahabad, I would prefer to rejoin my tenured job. I received a positive reply. I resigned from my job in Udaipur and rejoined Allahabad in February 1986.

I got into my old work routine and completed my first book, *Attribution Theory and Research*, which was published by Wiley Eastern in 1988. The book included my conceptual and empirical papers on causal attribution as well as some papers by other colleagues. By that time, the Indian Council of Social Science Research (ICSSR) had also sanctioned my research project on

Coping with Tragic Life Events. My colleagues and I began studies of patients afflicted by different chronic diseases and were recuperating in local hospitals.

During that period, I went to IIT Bombay for a colloquium and explored whether I could be offered a faculty position there. I was asked to meet the psychology faculty in the department, and they confidentially recommended that I would be offered a position. Within a fortnight of my return, I received the appointment letter. Given that the HSS department was on the third floor without any facility of an elevator, I very reluctantly declined the offer. This decision was also facilitated by the UGC Career Award for three years for undertaking research of my choice.

My career award project was on 'lotus in the mud', that is, how some children from the unprivileged background outperform other children in the school? What psychological attributes good performers have? I was trying to develop an educational resourcefulness model to train children for inculcating these attributes. In our initial survey, three critical attributes of resourcefulness were identified: self-esteem, sense of personal control, and planfullness. To test resourcefulness of children from deprived background, we developed a test in which a child was asked, 'suppose you are lost in a thick forest, what will you do?' Whatever option the child gave was discounted or ruled out by the interviewer, and this process continued till the child exhausted all the possibilities. The point was to observe how far the child might keep on going for inventing alternative solutions. The other question was 'suppose you fall in the river and do not know how to swim, what will you do?' There were five such scenarios with appropriate questions. The idea was to see how many options would the child think of? We interviewed a few children who were performing well in school. Ananta, a former graduate from the department, was a very creative research assistant, and she developed a large number of five-point rating scales. She created a fruit scale (e.g. taking guavas of uniformly bigger sizes and taught children that the lowest size of guava is numbered 1, and the largest one as 5). Sometimes she asked children to arrange guavas in increasing order of size and give them appropriate number. It was fun for children to learn the concept of rating scale. At the end of the interview session, the children and the interviewer could merrily feast on the rating scale. Such scales could be made of fruits, vegetables, pieces of wood, stones, etc.

One day Ananta interviewed a child and prepared a poetic version of the transcription. She recited it to me. When she asked the child what facilities he had in his house for studies, the child remained silent, cast his glance downward, and murmured that he lived in a single-room cottage with his family, where there was no space to study inside the house. When asked, who teaches you at home? He haltingly said that both his parents and brother were labourers and went to work early. Similar were his other responses to other questions and the pathos in his tone was obvious. Clearly, asking such questions only accentuated his sense of deprivation. The poem Ananta composed was so touching that I could not sleep that night. I felt guilty of heightening the sense of deprivation of the unprivileged, though the questions we asked were typically the same which are normally asked in such research. We had taken prior permission from the school authorities and the class teacher to interview children but such consent is routinely given in all cases. My discomfort was that we obtain data, write papers, and get our promotion or other rewards but what do these children get in return? I kept struggling with this issue without getting a clear answer. This kind of research was increasingly putting me off.

It is not that I completely stopped that type of research. I sporadically did engage in such data collection, particularly for the ICACBR rural research project. But gradually I was getting more involved in qualitative research, particularly in narrative research. In such research, I had a chance to sit and talk to the respondent in an informal setting, without having any prepared questionnaire. The narratives were then analysed from the respondents' point of view; sharing and building interpretations with them. I was finding this kind of narrative research much more involving and mutually rewarding for both the researcher and the respondent. I also encouraged my doctoral students to take up such constructionist approach in their research.

The hospital studies we completed during that period got published in good journals. These studies focussed on the causal attributions patients made for their chronic illness and the way such causal attributions helped them in coping with their own health crises. In general, patients frequently attributed their disease to God, Karma, fate, and their own carelessness. Among the multiple Hindu Gods, patients had their preferences. Indian patients avoided blaming family and others while attributing the causes of their illnesses. Interestingly, when we asked patients an open-ended question about the causes of their disease, metaphysical factors were not listed in the first place. They were mentioned only when the patients were specifically asked to rate them, both as causal and as recovery factors. We also developed a comprehensive measure of psychological recovery of hospital patients and found its positive linkages with some causal attributions, though not with medical recovery. This finding got me more interested in cultural factors in recovering from health crises.

A significant outcome of the foregoing period of research was an offer from the UNESCO to write a history of academic psychology in India. For this UNESCO project, I travelled to Delhi to consult UGC and CSIR for old reports, documents, and data. I wished to pattern my chapter differently from Prof D. Sinha's (1986) 'Psychology in a Third World Country'. However, the major problem was of finding the relevant information about the recent trends in psychological research in India. I scanned ICSSR research surveys in psychology and also obtained material from scattered sources.

In 1991, the Queen's University of Canada was awarded a major project on community-based rehabilitation of disabled by the Canadian International Development Agency and they were looking for a collaborating institution from India. Prof John Berry, who was part of the team, had frequently visited Allahabad in the past and had a close connection with Prof D. Sinha. Thus, our department became a natural choice for collaboration. The team stayed in the department for few days and we worked out modalities of the partnership. A small unit was constituted in the department under my charge. In summer, Prof D. Sinha and I went to Kingston for the first board meeting, where the International Centre for the Advancement of Community-based Rehabilitation (ICACBR) was formalized and its structure and programme activities were chalked out. There were seven institutions as its member organizations—four from Canada, two from India, and one each from Bangladesh and Indonesia. It was my first experience of being part of the apex body of an international institute and I was learning how major international projects worked. I stayed in Kingston for a month to plan research projects on disability attitudes with Prof Berry. That was the time I tried to understand what community-based rehabilitation (CBR) meant. My hospital studies came handy in planning research in the area of CBR in which part of the focus was on cultural beliefs about physical and neural disabilities.

In the initial stage, I travelled with the rest of the group to Mumbai, Bangalore, Solo (Indonesia), and Kingston to educate ourselves in the field of disability rehabilitation. We visited hospitals, rehabilitation centres, community projects, and advocacy groups. There were meetings organized with government officials, NGOs, and funding agencies. How much I learned about CBR and its philosophy and functioning is debatable! Nevertheless, the CBR project did turn me into an international traveller. In all those trips, we were discussing research, evaluation, and field projects to be funded by ICACBR. Most of those CBR projects looked like showcasing them for international visitors. These were prosthetic centres, vocational rehabilitation centres, and self-employment schemes run by local NGOs. We had a series of meetings in Mumbai and Allahabad, where members of other partner organizations also joined. Beside sporadic serious discussions, mostly these meetings were project tourism, eating in five-star hotels, and having a good time.

During the Dhaka trip in 1992, a fierce debate ensued about the purpose of this international CBR project and what we had been achieving. Bangladesh had a strong social service tradition with a large number of NGOs engaged in community services. There was a perception that the Western model of social work was diluting their tradition of social work. Western service organizations have a formal structure with laid down rules and regulations, and professional activities. Local traditional organizations valued more dedication and spirit of service within the socio-religious framework. On the second day of our conference, many students from Dhaka University barged in our hotel, inquiring about our purpose of coming to Dhaka. They were suspicious of our activities and heckled us. Being an Indian was no respite for me.

Dr Namita Pande and I started a CBR demonstration project at Sirathu, a place 75 km from Allahabad. We organized a series of meetings with local people and organized programmes for people with disability. We started an integrated school, organized loan melas, training programmes for self-employment and medical camps for disability certificates, and other similar activities. For this purpose, rather than taking money from ICACBR, we mobilized our own resources and grants from the Rajiv Gandhi Foundation. In all CBR projects, the core idea of rehabilitation of people with disability with the support of local communities appeared a far cry. Interestingly, none of the Western countries adopted CBR as a viable model for themselves but joined hands to promote it in poor countries. They could find many collaborators in India and elsewhere. As I observed in eight years of working with the ICACBR programmes, such as CBR, I had an implicit goal to perpetuate the Western hegemony in the developing world. It is unsurprising, therefore, that the CBR had lost its sheen and was hardly talked about in the international circuit in the last 10–15 years.

An important event during this period was an offer of residency at the Rockefeller Center, Bellagio, Italy for five weeks. My proposal to write chapters based on hospital studies during Bellagio residency was approved and I was there in the summer of 1992. The scenic beauty of the place and the stimulating environment had a profound effect on me. I came back fully rejuvenated.

My earlier hospital studies and projects on coping with tragic life events took a new turn. I was getting more and more interested in Indian folk tradition of health, healing, and well-being. Healing implies complete (including psycho-social) recovery from ill effects of a health crisis or a tragic life experience. Whether faith healing is scientific or not can be debated but its efficacy in recovering from mental and physical health problems is empirically verifiable. Faith healing is primarily psychological treatment of physical and mental problems. I wanted to extend Prof Sudhir Kakar's pioneering work in this area. I have been writing and talking about faith healing in many seminars and conferences.

In those days there was an offer from Sage India to prepare a series of volumes on best contributions by Indian psychologists since Independence. This project grew from a joint proposal by Prof G. Misra and myself, which we submitted to Sage India. We sent them a list of papers which we wanted to include in that volume. Mr Tejeshwar Singh was the then Chairman of Sage

India. He offered us to bring out a series of volumes in different areas, instead of only one area of psychology. Our first volume came out in 2002. However, we could not bring out other volumes in time. Our second volume came out in 2011 and by that time Sage India had lost interest in the project.

The department has been publishing a Sage journal *Psychology and Developing Societies* since 1989. Prof D. Sinha was the chief editor and Prof Tripathi was the editor of the journal in initial years. In 2000, I took over as the editor of the journal. The journal aimed to promote psychological indigenous research from developing countries. The idea was to encourage research based on concepts, theories, models and methods, focussing on the problems and concerns of non-Western countries. Our editorial team made efforts to improve the visibility and quality of published articles; we brought out special issues, and personally approached researchers for articles. We noticed that the Indians who publish in good journals outside did not send their best papers to the journal, nor did they take our 'rejection' decision on seemingly poor quality manuscripts in good spirit. Declining level of quality research in India was another limiting factor. Our editorial team had to constantly struggle to find good reviewers to evaluate the submitted papers. We were able to sustain and stabilize the journal but only marginally succeeded in improving its content and visibility. At the end of 2012, I handed over the reign of the journal back to Prof Tripathi.

I visited Calcutta University in March 2006 to give a series of lectures on qualitative methods in the Department of Anthropology. While delivering my first lecture, I found that my right hand was getting out of my control and then it suddenly went limp. I realized that it might be a stroke which had affected my right side. Although I continued my talk, my voice was gradually halting. After the audience was gone, I told Subha (the organizer of my talks) that I could not get up from my chair. On seeing my plight, a doctor came and she declared that it was indeed a stroke. I was rushed to the emergency ward of the local hospital. Fortunately, my wife Jyoti was with me. I had to undergo a brain surgery for a clot which took me about six months to recover. Thereafter I was confined to the wheelchair for my movement.

In 2004, I went to Puducherry to attend a major conference on Indian psychology. Around 200 researchers from India and abroad participated in the conference, many of whom I knew personally, or through their work. Indian psychology is primarily understood as the science of yoga and consciousness. My work on the folk traditions of healing barely figured in the broader frame of Indian psychology. However, attending that conference was a turning point for my research and teaching. I continued working in the area of indigenous healing as a core field of Indian psychology. Two years later, it was a pleasant surprise for me when Prof Rao asked me to be an editor, along with him and Prof Paranjpe, of the first *Handbook of Indian Psychology*. This handbook was published by the Cambridge University Press in 2008, in which many national and international scholars contributed chapters. My role in bringing out this handbook was limited but it did give me a new cap of Indian psychology. I gave lectures on Indian psychology at many places, attended conferences, and wrote articles and book chapters. An article on 'Core and Context of Indian Psychology' by Prof Misra and me was much talked about. I offered a course on Indian psychology in the Department of Psychology, Allahabad, for a couple of years, but it could not be sustained. My recent book *Health Beliefs and Coping with Chronic Diseases* was a culmination of my long-term interest and research in this area.

Over the years, I have been getting convinced that qualitative research, particularly the narrative methodology, was the best approach to understanding folk tradition of health and well-being. Dr Ravi Priya, a faculty at IIT-K, and I have conducted many workshops on qualitative research at different places across the nation. Qualitative approach takes the position that social reality is a construction of human mind, often collective, which changes our thinking, feelings, and action tendencies. Such constructed reality shapes our experiences of suffering, happiness, achievement, alienation, and well-being. It is in this sense that our cultural, social, and personal beliefs play a major role in shaping our notion of health and well-being.

Of late, my interest gradually shifted from the narrative method to first-person methods. To me, research in psychology has to take a u-turn—understanding the self (first) before understanding the other (third) person. Modern psychology modelled on physical sciences has primarily focussed on the study of the other person, referred to as the participant or the respondent. The dictum of first 'know thyself' was the ethos of all ancient societies. Modern psychology as a science had its beginning in the Wundtian method of introspection, which was later completely discarded in favour of the objective methods of experiment and testing. That was more than a century back, and since then first-person methods have become far more advanced and can deal with subjective–objective dichotomy in research. There is much scope to further develop yoga as a method of knowing about the inner state of the self and consciousness. Eastern human sciences are replete with such methodologies to study mind and emotions. This could be an exciting and challenging area of research in psychology in the times to come.

As I am aging my interest is shifting from the study of hospital patients toward the viability of integrating folk healing, Indian system of medicine, and modern medicine within the healthcare programme of India. I have been looking at the Ayurvedic and folk traditions, which are based on different premises and principles of healing, but have complimented each other in the long history. There is a similar conflicting scenario between modern medicine and indigenous systems in India in the present times. I wrote six essays dealing with this complex issue and have sent the book to Sage India, who is now publishing it. Prof Misra and I have also brought out a book on a collection of select papers of Prof Sinha, adding to it his biographical sketch. All this is the terminal part of my journey as a faculty at the Department of Psychology, University of Allahabad.

I am no one to judge the worth of my academic journey so far. I often ask myself: How far have I come in my quest to understand the human life? Being in academic psychology for the last 40 years, do I have a better understanding about myself and people around me than before? I am still struggling to answer the same basic questions that had brought me to psychology. Although my quest to understand the human puzzle continues, I am gratified that the self is always a work in progress, and that the University of Allahabad provided me with the opportunity to serve and realize this truth that nothing is conclusive in science.

References

Adair, J. (1990, July). *Indicators of indigenization and development of the discipline in developing countries.* Paper presented at the International Congress of Cross-cultural Psychology, Nara, Japan.

Adair, J.G. (1989). *Indigenous developments in Indian psychology: A quantitative assessment.* Paper presented at the Annual Meeting of the Canadian Psychological Association, Halifax, Nova Scotia.

Adair, J.G., Pandey, J., Begam, H.A., Puhan, B.N. and Vohra, N. (1995). Indigenization and development of the discipline: Perceptions and opinions of Indian and Bangladeshi Psychologists. *Journal of Cross-Cultural Psychology*, 26, 392–407.

Adair, J.G., Puhan, B.N. and Vohra, N. (1993). Indigenization of psychology: Empirical assessment of progress in Indian research. *International Journal of Psychology*, 29, 149–69.

Agrawal, K.G. (1973). Psychology or adoptology. *Social Scientist*, 1, 1–4.

American Psychologist. (January 2004). Special issue on health and spirituality/religion.

Anand, J. (2011). *Healing Narratives of Women: A Psychological Perspective*. Jaipur: Rawat Publications.

Anand, J. (2006). Toward a conceptual formulation of psychological healing. *Psychological Studies*, 51(2). 119–25.

Anand, J. (2004). Working through emotional pain: A narrative study of the healing process. *Psychological Studies*, 49, 185–92.

Anant, S.S. (1970). Caste prejudices and its perception by harijans. *Journal of Social Psychology*, 82, 271–78.

Ansari, Z.A. (1990). Pakistan. In G. Shouksmith and E.A. Shouksmith (Eds), *Psychology in Asia and the Pacific*. Bangkok: UNESCO.

Asch, S.E. (1951). Effect of group pressure upon the modification and distortion of judgement. In H. Guetzkow (Ed.), *Groups, Leadership and Men*. Pittsburgh: Carnegie.

Atal, Y. (1976). *Social Sciences: The Indian Scene*. New Delhi: Abhinav Prakashan.

Banerjee, M.N. (1932). A study of the increase of subjective brightness in a circumscribed field. *Indian Journal of Psychology*, 7, 76–81.

Barnes, B. (1974). *Scientific Knowledge and Sociological Theory*. London: Routledge & Kegan Paul.

Barnett, W.L. (1955). Survey of research with psychological tests in India. *Psychological Bulletin*, 52, 105–21.

Basham, A.L. (1954). *The Wonder that was India*. New York: Grove Press.

Begam, H. (1990). Bangladesh. In G. Shouksmith and E.A. Shouksmith (Eds), *Psychology in Asia and the Pacific*. Bangkok: UNESCO.

Berry, J. (1980). Social and cultural change: In H.C. Triandis and R. Brislin (Eds), *Handbook of Cross-Cultural Psychology*, Vol. 5 (pp. 221–79). Boston: Allyn & Bacon.

Berry, J., Poortinga, Y., Segall, M. and Dasen, P. (1992). *Cross-Cultural Psychology: Research and Applications*. Cambridge, England: Cambridge University Press.

Berry, J.W. (1989). Imposed etics-emics-derived etics: The operationalization of a compelling idea. *International Journal of Psychology*, 24, 721–35.

Bhatia, S. (2002). Orientalism in Euro-American and Indian psychology: Historical representation of "natives" in colonial and postcolonial contexts. *History of Psychology*, 5(4), 376–98.

Bhawuk, D.P.S. (2008a) Anchoring cognition, emotion, and behavior in desire: A model from the *Bhagavad-Gita*. In K.R. Rao, A.C. Paranjpe, and A.K. Dalal (Eds), *Handbook of Indian Psychology* (pp. 390–413). New Delhi, India: Cambridge University Press.

Bhawuk, D.P.S. (2008b). Science of culture and culture of science: Worldview and choice of conceptual models and methodology. *The Social Engineer*, 11(2), 26–43.

Bhawuk, D.P.S. (2005). A model of self, work, and spirituality from the *Bhagavad-Gita:* Implications for self-efficacy, goal setting, and global psychology. In K.R. Rao and S.B. Marwaha (Eds), *Toward a Spiritual psychology: Essays in Indian Psychology* (pp. 41–71). New Delhi: Samvad Indian Foundation.

Bhawuk, D.P.S. (2003). Culture's influence on creativity: The case of Indian spirituality. *International Journal of Intercultural Relations*, 27 (1), 1–22.

Bhawuk, D.P.S. (1999). Who attains peace: An Indian model of personal harmony. *Indian Psychological Review*, 52(2 and 3), 40–48.

Blackler, F. (Ed.). (1983). *Social Psychology and Developing Countries.* Chichester, London: Sage.

Bondurant, J.V. (1965). *Conquest of Violence: The Gandhian Philosophy of Conflict.* Berkeley and Los Angles: University of California Press.

Bose, G.C. (1939). Progress of psychology in India during the past twenty-five years. In B. Prasad (Ed.), *The Progress of Science in India during the Last Twenty-Five Years* (pp. 336–52). Calcutta: Indian Science Congress.

Botterill, George. (1989). Human nature and folk psychology in the person and the human mind: Issues. In *Ancient and Modern Philosophy*. New York: Clarendon Press.

Buss, A.R. (1975). The emerging field of the sociology of psychological knowledge. *American Psychologist*, 30, 988–1002.

Carstairs, G.M. (1957). *The Twice Born.* London: Hogarth Press.

Chakraborty, S.K. (1995). *Ethics in Management: Vedantic Perspectives.* New Delhi: Oxford University Press.

Chakraborty, S.K. (1987). *Managerial Effectiveness and Quality of Worklife: Indian Insights.* New Delhi: Tata McGraw-Hill.

Chatterjee, R.G. (1954). An investigation on the perceptual side of repression. *Indian Journal of Psychology*, 29, 191–93.

Cohen, D. and Cohen, S. (1977). *Psychologists on Psychology*. London: Routledge & Kegan Paul.

Cornelissen, M., Misra, G. and Varma, S. (2011). *Foundations of Indian Psychology*. New Delhi: Pearson.

Dalal, A.K. (2016). *Cultural Psychology of Health in India*. New Delhi: Sage India.

Dalal, A.K. (2015). *Health Beliefs and Coping with Chronic Diseases.* New Delhi: Sage India.

Dalal, A.K. (2010). Psychosocial interventions in community development. In G. Misra (Ed.), *Fifth Survey of Research in Psychology*. New Delhi: Pearson.

Dalal, A.K. (2002). Psychology in India: A historical introduction. In G. Misra and A.K. Mohanty (Eds), *Perspectives on Indigenous Psychology*. New Delhi: Concept.

Dalal, A.K. (2001). Health psychology. In J. Pandey (Ed.), *Psychology in India Revisited: Development in the Discipline* (pp. 356–411). New Delhi: Sage.

Dalal, A.K. (1990). India. In G. Shouksmith and E.A. Shouksmith (Eds), *Psychology in Asia and the Pacific*. Bangkok: UNESCO.

Dalal, A.K. (1988). *Attribution Theory and Research*. New Delhi: Wiley Eastern.

Dalal, A.K. (1986). A science in search of its identity: Twentieth century psychology in India. *Indian Psycholigical Abstract and Reviews,* 3 (2), 201–44.

Dalal, A.K. and Misra, G. (2011). *New Direction in Health Psychology*. New Delhi: Sage India.

Dalal, A.K. and Misra, G. (2006). Psychology of health and well-being: Some emerging perspectives. *Psychological Studies*, 51 (2 and 3), 91–104.

Dalal, A.K. and Priya, R. (2015). Introduction to qualitative research. In R.K. Priya and A.K. Dalal (Eds), *Qualitative Research on Illness, Well-Being and Self-Growth* (pp. 1–22). New Delhi: Routledge.

Dalal, A.K. and Sharma, R. (1990). *Sample and Method in Social and Personality Research: Content Analysis of Psychological Abstracts*. Unpublished manuscript, University of Allahabad, Allahabad.

Dalal, A.S. (2000). *Greater Psychology*. Pondicherry: Sri Aurobindo Ashram.

Das, J.P. (1962). Learning under conditions of hypnotically induced anxiety and non-anxiety. *International Journal of Clinical and Experimental Hypnosis*, 10, 163–68.

Davar, B.V. (1999). *Mental Health of Indian Women: A Feminist Agenda*. New Delhi: Sage.

Davids, C.A.F.R. (1936/1978). *The Birth of Indian Psychology and its Development in Buddhism*. New Delhi: Munshiram Manoharlal Publications, reprint Oriental Books.

Depraz, N. (1999). Phenomenological reduction as praxis. In F.J. Varela and J. Shear (Eds), *The View from Within*. Exerter: Imprint Academic.

DeRidder, R. and Tripathi, R.C. (Eds). (1992). *Norm Violation and Intergroup Relations*. Oxford: Clarendon Press.

Derrida, J. (1982). *Margins of Philosophy* (translated by A. Boss) Chicago: Chicago University Press.

Dhanagare, D.N. (1993). *Themes and Perspectives in Indian Sociology*. Jaipur: Rawat Publications.

Dhanagare, D.N. (1985). India. In Y. Atal (Ed.), *UNESCO Reports: Sociology and Social Anthropology in the Asia and Pacific*. New Delhi: Wiley Eastern.

Dharampal. (2000). *The Beautiful Tree: Indigenous Indian Education in the Eighteenth Century*. Mapusa, Goa: The Other India Press.

Dosajh, D.N.L. (1953). A psychological study of various tensions prevalent among refugees residing in Ahmedabad area. *Indian Journal of Psychology*, 57, 79–84.

Dube, S.C. (1984). India. In Y. Atal (Ed.), *Social Sciences in Asia and the Pacific*. Paris: UNESCO.

Elnagar, M.M., Mitra, P. and Rao, M.N. (1971). Mental health in an Indian rural community. *British Journal of Psychiatry*, 118, 499–504.

Enriquez, V.G. (1993). Developing a Filipino psychology. In U. Kim and J.W. Berry (Eds), *Indigenous Psychologies: Research and Experience in Cultural Context* (pp. 152–69). Newbury Park, CA: Sage.

Flanagan, O.J. Jr. (1981). Psychology, progress and problems of reflexivity: A study in the epistemological foundations of psychology. *Journal of the History of Behavioral Science*, 17, 375–86.

Foucault, M. (1977). *The Archaeology of Knowledge*. London: Tavistock.

Ganguli, H.C. (1971). Psychological research in India: 1920–1967. *International Journal of Psychology*, 6, 165–77.

Ganguli, H.C. (1961). *Industrial Productivity and Motivation*. Bombay: Asia Publishing House.

Geddes, A. (1947). The social and psychological significance of variability in population change with examples from India, 1871–1941. *Human Relations*, 1, 181–205.

Gergen, K.J. (2009). *Relational Being*. New York: Oxford University Press.

Gergen, K.J. (2007). *An Invitation to Social Construction*. London: Sage Publications.

Gergen, K.J. (1994). *Realities and Relationships: Sounding in Social Construction*. Cambridge: Harward University Press.

Gergen, K.J. (1989a). Realities and their relationships. In W.J. Baker and S. Tarwee (Eds), *Recent Trends in Theoretical Psychology* (pp. 51–62). New York: Springer–Verlag.

Gergen, K.J. (1989b). Social psychology and the wrong revolution. *European Journal of Social Psychology*, 19, 463–84.

Gergen, K.J., Gulerce, A., Lock, A. and Misra, G. (1996). Psychological science in cultural context. *American Psychologist*, 51, 496–503.

Gilgin, A.R. and Gilgin, C.K. (Eds). (1987). *Psychology in World Perspective: International Handbook of Psychology*. Westport, CT: Greenwood Press.

Goleman, D. (2004). *Destructive Emotions: A Scientific Dialogue with the Dalai Lama*. NY: Bantam Dell.

Guha, B. (1998). *Conflict and Violence in Indian society*. New Delhi: Kanishka Publishing House.

Heron, J. (1996). *Cooperative Inquiry: Research into the Human Conditions*. London: Sage.

Hofstede, G. (1980). *Culture's Consequences: International Differences in Work-Related Values*. Beverly Hills, CA: Sage

Holzner, B. (1968). *Reality Construction in Society*. Cambridge, MA. Schenkman Publishing.

Horsburgh, H.J.N. (1968). *Non-Violence and Aggression: A Study of Gandhi's Moral Equivalent of War*. London: Oxford University Press.

ICSSR. (1994). *Computer Listing of Indian Psychologists*. New Delhi: ICSSR Archives.

Jain, A.K. (2005). Psychology in India. *British Psychologist*, 16, 206–08.

Jain, L.C. (1986). *Grass Without Roots: Rural Development Under Government Auspecies*. New Delhi: Sage.

Jain, U. (1978). Competition tolerance in high and low density urban and rural areas. *Journal of Social Psychology*, 105, 297–98.

James, W. (1890). *The Principles of Psychology*, in two volumes. New York: Henry Holt and Company.

Joshi, K. and Cornelissen, M. (2004). *Consciousness, Indian Psychology and Yoga*. New Delhi: Centre for Studies in Civilizations.

Kakar, S. (2008). *Mad and Divine*. New Delhi: Penguin.

Kakar, S. (2003). Psychoanalysis and Eastern spiritual traditions. *Journal of Analytic Psychology*, 48, 659–78.

Kakar, S. (1996). *The Indian Psyche*. New Delhi: Oxford University Press.

Kakar, S. (1991). *The Analyst and Mystic*. London: Penguin.

Kakar, S. (1982a). *Inner World: A Psycho-Analytic Study of Childhood and Society in India.* New Delhi: Oxford University Press.

Kakar, S. (1982b). *Shamans, Mystics and Doctors: A Psychological Inquiry into India and its Healing Traditions*. New Delhi: Oxford University Press.

Kakar, S. (1978). *The Inner Experience*. New Delhi: Oxford University Press.

Kakar, S. (1971). The themes of authority in social relations in India. *Journal of Social Psychology*, 84, 93–101.

Kakar, S. and Kakar, K. (2007). *The Indians: Portrait of a People*. New Delhi: Penguin Books.

Kakar, S. and Ross, J. (1986). *Tales of Love, Sex and Danger*. New Delhi: Oxford University Press.

Kanekar, S. (1988). Attribution of causal and moral responsibility: The case of a rape victim. In A.K. Dalal (Ed.), *Attribution Theory and Research*. New Delhi: Wiley Eastern.

Khandawalla, P. (1988). Organizational effectiveness. In J. Pandey (Ed.), *Psychology in India: The State-of-the-Art* (pp. 97–215). New Delhi: Sage.

Kim, U. and Berry, J.W. (Eds). (1993). *Indigenous Psychologies: Research and Experience in Cultural Context* (pp. 152–69). Newbury Park, CA: Sage.

Kothurkar, V.K. (1972). Experimental psychology. In S.K. Mitra (Ed.), *A Survey of Research in Psychology*. Bombay: Popular Prakashan.

Krishnamurti, J. (1976). *Freedom from the Known*. Francisco: Harper San Francisco.

Krishnan, L. (2005). Concepts of social behaviour in India: Daan and distributive justice. *Psychological Studies*, 50(1) 21–31.

Kumar, M. (2006). Rethinking psychology in India: Debating pasts and futures. *Annual Review of Critical Psychology*, 5. Retrieved from www.discourseunit.com/arcp/5.

Kumar, S.K.K. (2008). Indian thought and tradition: A psycho-historical perspective. In K.R. Rao, A.C. Paranjpe and A.K. Dalal (Eds), *Handbook of Indian Psychology* (pp. 19–52). New Delhi: Cambridge University Press.

Kumar, S.K.K. (2005). Development of indigenous Indian perspective. In G. Misra (Ed.), *Fifth Survey of Research in Psychology*, Vol. 1. New Delhi: Sage.

Kuppuswami, B. (1985). *Elements of Ancient Indian Psychology*. New Delhi: Vikas Publishing House.

Loomba, R.M. (1946). Psychological conditions of peace. *Indian Journal of Psychology*, 21, 77–80.

Macaulay, T.B. (1972). Minute on Indian education. In T.B. Macaulay, *Selected Writings* (pp. 237–51). (J. Clive and T. Pinney, Eds). Chicago: University of Chicago Press. (Original "Minute" presented in 1835).

Mannaheim, K. (1940). *Man and Society in the Age of Reconstruction* (translated by E. Shils). New York: Appleton-Century.

Mays, N. and Pope, C. (1995). Rigour and qualitative research. *British Medical Journal*, 311, 109–12.

McClelland, D.C. (1961). *The Achieving Society*. Princeton: Van Nostrand.

McClelland, D.C. and Winter (1969). *Motivating economic achievement*. New York: Free Press.

Mehta, P. (1975). *Election Campaign*. Delhi: National Publishing House.

Menon, S. (2005). What is Indian psychology: Transcendence in and while thinking. *Journal of Transpersonal Psychology*, 37(2), 83–98.

Merton, R.K. (1968). *Social Theory and Social Structure*. New York: The Free Press.

Miller, J.G. (1998). Theoretical issues in cultural psychology and social constructionism. In J.W. Berry, Y. Poortinga, and J. Pandey (Eds), *Handbook of Cross-Cultural Psychology: Theoretical and Methodological Perspectives,* Vol. 1. Boston: Allyn & Bacon.

Minturn, A. and Hitchock, P. (1966). The Rajputs of Khalapur. In R. Whiting (Ed.), *Six Cultures*. Cambridge, MA: Harvard University Press.

Misra, G. (2007). *Psychology and Societal Development: Paradigmatic and Social Concerns*. New Delhi: Concept.

Misra, G. (2005). The science of affect: Some Indian insights In K.R. Rao and S. Bhatt–Marwah (Eds), *Towards a Spiritual Psychology: Essays in Indian Psychology* (pp. 229–48). New Delhi: Samvad India Foundation.

Misra G. (2004). Emotion in modern psychology and Indian thought. In K. Joshi and M. Cornelissen (Eds) *Consciousness, Science Society and Yoga*. New Delhi: Centre for the Studies of Civilization.

Misra, G. (1986). A factor analytic study of achievement and means: An Indian view. *International Journal of Psychology*, 19, 717–31.

Misra, G. (1982). *Deprivation and Development: A Review of Indian Studies*. New Delhi: Concept.

Misra, G. and Gergen, K.J. (1993). On the place of culture in psychological science. *International Journal of Psychology*, 28, 225–43.

Misra, G. and Kumar, S. (2008). Psychology in India: Retrospect and prospect. In G. Misra (Ed.) *Psychology in India: Advances in Research,* Vol. 4. New Delhi: Pearson education.

Misra, G. and Mohanty, A. (2002). *Perspectives on Indigenous Psychology.* New Delhi: Concept.

Misra, G. and Tripathi, K.N. (2004). Psychological dimensions of poverty and deprivation. In J. Pandey (Ed.), *Psychology in India Revisited: Development in the Discipline,* Vol. 3. New Delhi: Sage.

Misra, G. and Tripathi, L.B. (1980). *Psychological Consequences of Prolonged Deprivation.* Agra: National Psychological Corporation.

Misra, G. (Ed.). (2014). Psychology and psychoanalysis. In the Series on *History of Science, Philosophy and Culture,* Vol. IX, General Editor: D.P. Chattopadhyaya. New Delhi: ICPR.

Misra, G. (Ed.). (2010). *Fifth Survey of Research in Psychology,* Vol. 3. New Delhi: Pearson.

Misra, G., Prakash, A. and Verma, S. (1999). Psychology in India: Perceptions and perspectives. *Psychology and Developing Societies,* 11, 25–53.

Mitra, S.K. (1972). Psychological research in India. In S.K. Mitra (Ed.), *A Survey of Research in Psychology.* Bombay: Popular Prakashan.

Moghaddam, F.M. (1987). Psychology in the three worlds. *American Psychologist,* 42, 912–20.

Mohanty, A. (1982). Bilingualism among Kond tribals: Consequences, issues and implications. *Indian Psychologist,* 1, 34–43.

Murlidharan, R. (1971). *Developmental Norms of Indian Children of 2 Years to 5 Years.* New Delhi: NCERT.

Murphy, G. (1953). *In the Minds of Men.* New York: Basic Books.

Murthy, H.N. (1980). Counseling and psychotherapy. In U. Pareek (Ed.), *A Survey of Research in Psychotherapy: 1971–1976* (Part 1). Mumbai: Popular Prakashan.

Muthayya, B.C. (1982). Psycho-social study of rural disadvantaged: A psycho-social study in Punjab and Madhya Pradesh. *Journal of Rural Development,* 15, 143–260.

Naidu, P.S. (1947). Psychology and the rehabilitation of human society. *Indian Journal of Psychology,* 22, 1–24.

Nakamura, H. (1964). *Ways of Thinking of Eastern Peoples: India, China, Tibet and Japan.* (English Translation). Hawaii: East West Center Press.

Nandy, A. (1995). *The Savage Freud and Other Essays on Possible and Retrievable Selves.* New Delhi: Oxford University Press.

Nandy, A. (1983). *The Intimate Enemy: Loss and Recovery of Self under Colonialism*. New Delhi: Oxford University Press.

Nandy, A. (1982). *Psychology of Colonialism: Sex, Age and Ideology in British India*. New Delhi: Oxford University Press.

Nandy, A. (1974). The non-paradigmatic crisis in Indian psychology: Reflection on a recipient culture of science. *Indian Journal of Psychology*, 49, 1–20.

Nandy, A. (Ed.). (1988). *Science, Hegemony and Violence: A Requiem for Modernity*. New Delhi: Oxford University Press.

NCERT. (1981). *Psychological Tests in India*. New Delhi: NCERT.

NCERT (1968). *The Third Indian Yearbook of Education*. New Delhi: NCERT.

Neki, J.S. (1973). Guru–chela relationship: The possibility of a therapeutic paradigm. *American Journal of Orthopsychiatry*, 43, 755–66.

Nijhawan, N.K. (1983). *Directory of Social Scientists*. New Delhi: ICSSR.

Owusu-Bempah, K. and Howitt, D. (2000). *Psychology Beyond Western Perspectives*. Leicester, England: British Psychological Society Books.

Padaki, R. (1988). Job attitudes. In J. Pandey (Ed.), *Psychology in India: The State-of-the-Art* (pp. 19–95). New Delhi: Sage.

Pal, G. (1936). Difference limen for continuous change of lifted weight under different attitudes. *Indian Journal of Psychology*, 12, 255–71.

Palsane, M.N., Bhavsagar, S.N., Goswami, R.P. and Evans, G.W. (1986). The concept of stress in the Indian tradition. *Journal of Indian Psychology*, 5, 1–12.

Pande, N. and Naidu, R.K. (1992). Anasakti and health: A study of non-attachment. *Psychology and Developing Societies*, 4(1), 89–104.

Pandey, J. (2004). Psychology in India enters the twenty-first century: Movement toward an indigenous discipline. In J. Pandey (Ed.) *Psychology in India Revisited: Developments in the Discipline*, Vol. 3 (pp. 342–70). New Delhi: Sage.

Pandey, J. (1986). Social-cultural perspectives on ingratiation. In B.A. Mahar and W.B. Mahar (Eds), *Progress in Experimental Personality Research*, Vol. 14. New York: Academic Press.

Pandey, J. (Ed.). (2002). *Psychology in India Revisited*, Vol. 2. New Delhi: Sage.

Pandey, J. (Ed.). (2001). *Psychology in India Revisited*, Vol. 1. New Delhi: Sage.

Pandey, J. (Ed.). (1988). *Psychology in India: The State-of-the Art*, Vols. 1, 2, 3. New Delhi: Sage.

Pandey, J. and Singh, P. (2005). Social psychology in India: Social roots and development. *International Journal of Psychology*, 40, 239–53.

Pandey, R.E. (1969). Psychology in India. *American Psychologist*, 24, 936–39.

Paranjpe, A.C. (2006). From tradition through colonialism to globalization: Reflections on the history of psychology in India. In A.C. Brock (Ed.). *Internationalizing the History of Psychology*. New York: New York University Press.

Paranjpe, A.C. (2002). Problems and prospects for an indigenous psychology in India. In G. Misra and A.K. Mohanty (Eds), *Perspectives on Indigenous Psychology*. New Delhi: Concept.

Paranjpe, A.C. (1998). *Self and Identity in Modern Psychology and Indian Thought*. New York: Plenum.

Paranjpe, A.C. (1984). *Theoretical Psychology: The Meeting of East and West*. New York: Plenum Press.

Paranjpe, A.C. (1970). *Caste Prejudice and Individual*. Mumbai: Lalvani.

Paranjpe, A.C., Ho, D.Y.F. and Rieber, R.W. (Eds). (1988). *Asian Contributions to Psychology*. New York: Praeger.

Pareek, U. (1981). *A Survey of Research in Psychology: 1971–1976, Part 2.* Bombay: Popular Prakashan.

Pareek, U. (1980). *A Survey of Research in Psychology: 1971–1976, Part 1.* Bombay: Popular Prakashan.

Pareek, U. (1967). Poverty and motivation: Figure and ground. In V.L. Allen (Ed.), *Psychology Factors in Poverty*. New York: Academic Press.

Pareek, U. and Rao, T.V. (1974a). *Handbook of Psychological and Social Instruments.* Baroda: Samashti.

Pareek, U. and Rao, T.V. (1974b). *A Status Study of Population Research in India: Behavioural Sciences,* Vol. 1. New Delhi: Tata McGraw Hill.

Pareek, U., Dixit, N. and Sarupariya, D. (1979). Psychologists in India. *Bombay Psychologist*, 2, 5–16.

Pelton, L.H. (1974). *The Psychology of Nonviolence*. New York: Pergamon Press.

Pestonjee, D.M. (1986). *Handbook of Psychological Tests*. Bombay: Popular Prakashan.

Prabhu, G.G. (1983). Clinical psychology then and now. *Indian Journal of Clinical Psychology*, 10, 1–16.

Prabhu, G.G. (1980). Deviance and pathology. In U. Pareek (Ed.), *A Survey of Research in Psychology* (pp. 257–332). Bombay: Popular Prakashan.

Prasad, J. (1935). The psychology of rumour: A study relating to the great Indian earthquake of 1934. *British Journal of Psychology*, 26, 1–15.

Premasiri, P.D. (2008). Verities of cognition in early Buddhism. In K.R. Rao, A.C. Paranjpe, and A.K. Dalal (Eds), *Handbook of Indian Psychology* (pp. 85–104). New Delhi: Cambridge University Press.

Priya, R.K. (2010). The research relationship as a facilitator of remoralization and self-growth: Postearthquake suffering and healing. *Qualitative Health Research*, 20(4), 479–95.

Puhan, B.N. (1995). Projective-inventory: An indigenous approach to personality assessment. *Psychology and Developing Societies*, 7(2), 115–31.

Puhan, B.N. (1994). *Psychological Testing in India*. Presidential address to the Vth Annual Convention of National Academy of Psychology (December 21–23), at Allahabad University, Allahabad.

Puhan, B.N. and Vohra, N. (1993). Indigenization of psychology: Psychological assessment of progress in Indian research. *International Journal of Psychology*, 28, 149–69.

Radhakrishnan, S. (1953). *The Principal Upanishads*. London: Allen & Unwin.

Ramasubban, R. (1977). Toward a relevant sociology of science in India. In S.S. Blume (Ed.), *Perspectives in Sociology of Science* (pp. 155–203). New York: John Wiley and Sons.

Rao, K.R. (2008). Prologue: Introducing Indian Psychology. In K.R. Rao, A.C. Paranjpe and A.K. Dalal (Eds), *Handbook of Indian Psychology* (pp. 1–18). New Delhi: Cambridge University Press.

Rao, K.R. (2005). Scope and substance of India psychology. In K.R. Rao and S.B. Marwaha (Eds), *Towards a Spiritual Psychology: Essays on Indian Psychology*. New Delhi: Samvad Indian Foundation.

Rao, K.R. (2002a). *Consciousness Studies: Cross-cultural Perspectives*. Jefferson, NC: McFarland.

Rao, K.R. (2002b). Consciousness studies: A survey of perspectives and research. In J. Pandey (Ed.), *Psychology in India Revisited,* Vol. 2 (pp. 19–162). New Delhi: Sage.

Rao, K.R. (1988). Psychology of transcendence: A study in early Buddhist psychology. In A.C. Paranjpe, D.Y.F. Ho, and R.W. Rieber (Eds), *Asian Contributions to Psychology*. New York: Praeger.

Rao, K.R. and Marwaha, S.B. (Eds). (2005). *Towards a Spiritual Psychology: Essays on Indian Psychology*. New Delhi: Samvad Indian Foundation.

Rao, K.R. and Paranjpe, A. (2015). *Psychology in the Indian Tradition*. New Delhi: Springer.

Rao, K.R. and Paranjpe, A.C. (2008). Yoga psychology: Theory and application. In K.R. Rao, A. Paranjpe and A.K. Dalal (Eds), *Handbook of Indian Psychology*. New Delhi: Cambridge University Press.

Rao, K.R., Paranjpe, A.C., and Dalal, A.K. (Eds). (2008). *Handbook of Indian Psychology*. New Delhi: Cambridge University Press.

Rao, R. (1983). The conception of stress in Indian thought: I. The theoretical aspects of stress in Samkhya and yoga systems and II. The practical involvement in Gita and Ayurveda. *NIMHANS Journal*, 1, 115–31.

Rao, R. (1962). *Development of Psychological Thought in India*. Mysore: Kavyalaya.

Rath, R. (1979). Reorientation of Teaching and Research in Indian Universities. UGC Panel Report, New Delhi.

Rath, R. and Sircar, N.C. (1960). Intercaste relationships as reflected in the study of attitudes and opinion of six Hindu caste groups. *Journal of Social Psychology*, 51, 3–25.

Sabini, J. and Silver, M. (1982). *Moralities of Everyday Life*. London: Oxford University Press.

Safaya, R. (1975). *Indian Psychology: A Critical and Historical Analysis of Psychological Speculation in India Philosophical Literature*. New Delhi: Munshiram Manoharlal.

Said, E. (1978). *Orientalism*. New York: Penguin.

Sarasvathi, S. (1982). Growing up in Varanasi. *Seminar*, 27, 22–25.

Sarasvathi, S. (1975). Socialization for competence. In J.W. Berry and Tunner (Eds), *Handbook of Cross-Cultural Psychology: Theoretical and Applied Cross-Cultural Psychology*. Amsterdam: Zeitlinger.

Saraswathi, T.S. (1999). *Culture, Socialization and Human Development: Theory, Research and Applications in India*. New Delhi: Sage.

Saraswathi, T.S. (1998). Many deities, one god: Toward convergence on cultural and cross-cultural psychology. *Culture and Psychology, 4,* 147–160.

Semin, G. and Chassein, J. (1985). The relationships between higher order models and everyday conceptions of personality. *European Journal of Social Psychology*, 15, 1–15.

Sen, I. (1986). *Integral Psychology: The Psychological System of Sri Aurobindo*. Pondicherry: Sri Aurobindo International Centre for Education.

Sengupta, N.N. and Sinha, C.P.N. (1926). Mental work in isolation and in group. *Indian Journal of Psychology*, 1, 106–10.

Sethi, B.B., Gupta, S.C., and Kumar, R. (1967). 300 urban families. *Indian Journal of Psychiatry*, 9, 280–302.

Sharma, S. (1999). *Quantum Rope: Science, Mysticism and Management.* New Delhi: New Age International.

Sharma, S. (1996). *Management in New Age: Western Windows Indian Doors.* New Delhi: New Age International.

Shweder, R.A. (1991). *Thinking through Cultures: Expeditions in Cultural Psychology.* Cambridge, MA: Harvard University Press.

Singh, A.K. (1983). Health modernity education in India. *Social Change*, 13, 27–34.

Singh, A.K. (1981). Development of religious identity and prejudice in Indian children. In D. Sinha (Ed.), *Socialization of the Indian child* (pp. 87–100). New Delhi: Concept Publishing Company.

Singh, A.K. and Dalal, A.K. (1988). Psychology in India: A survey of doctoral students. *International Journal of Psychology*, S3, 525–35.

Singh, K.K. (1969). *Patterns of Caste Tension.* Bombay: Asia Publishing House.

Singh, R. (1986). Two problems in cognitive algebra: Imputations and averaging-versus-multiplying. In N.H. Anderson (Ed.), *Contributions to Information Integration Theory.* New York: Academic Press.

Singh, R. and Singh, P. (1994). Prediction of performance using motivation and ability information: New light on integrational capacity and weighting strategies. *Cognitive Development*, 9, 455–96.

Singh, S.D. (1963). Effect of dexidine ephedrine phenobarbitone and chlor-promazine on the latency of autokinetic movement. *Psychological Studies*, 8, 7–14.

Singh-Sengupta, S. (2007). Transforming Organizations Through Raja Yoga. *Conference organized at Purvanchal University, Jaunpur. UP, during March 29–31.*

Singh, Y. (1986). *Indian Sociology: Social Conditioning and Emerging Concerns.* New Delhi: Vistar Publication.

Sinha, A.K.P. and Upadhyaya, O.P. (1960). Change and persistence in stereotypes of university students towards different ethnic groups during Sino-Indian border dispute. *Journal of Social Psychology*, 52, 31–39.

Sinha, D. (1998). Changing perspectives in social psychology in India: A journey towards indigenization. *Asian Journal of Social Psychology*, 1, 17–31.

Sinha, D. (1997). Indigenizing psychology. In J.W. Berry, Y. Poortinga and J. Pandey (Eds), *Handbook of Cross-Cultural Psychology: Theoretical and Methodological Perspectives,* Vol. 1. Boston: Allyn & Bacon.

Sinha, D. (1996a). Culturally rooted psychology in India: Dangers and developments. *International Journal of Psychology*, 30, 99–110.

Sinha, D. (1996b). Culture as the target and culture as the source: A review of cross-cultural psychology in Asia. *Psychology and Developing Societies*, 8(1), 83–105.

Sinha, D. (1994). Indigenisation of psychology in India. *Indian Psychological Abstracts and Reviews*, 1(1), 179–215.

Sinha, D. (1993). Indigenization of psychology in India and its relevance. In U. Kim and J.W. Berry (Eds), *Indigenous Psychologies* (pp. 30–43). London: Sage.

Sinha, D. (1986). *Psychology in a Third World Country: An Indian Experience*. New Delhi: Sage.

Sinha, D. (1983). Human assessement in Indian. In S.H. Ervine and J.N. Berry (Ed.), *Human Assessement and Cultural Factors* (pp. 17–33). New York: Plenum Press.

Sinha, D. (1981). Non-Western perspectives in psychology: Why, what and whiter? *Journal of Indian Psychology*, 3, 1–9.

Sinha, D. (1977). Scientist professional model in problem-oriented applied social psychology research. *Journal of Social and Economic Studies*, 5, 219–33.

Sinha, D. (1969). *Indian Villages in Transition: A Motivational Analysis.* New Delhi: Associated Publishing House.

Sinha, D. (1965). Integration of modern psychology with modern thought. In A.J. Sutchi and M.A. Vick (Eds), *Readings in Humanistic Psychology*. (pp. 265–79). New York: Free Press.

Sinha, D. (1952). Behaviour in a catastrophic situation: A psychological study of reports and rumours. *British Journal of Psychology*, 43, 200–309.

Sinha, D. and Tripathi, R.C. (1994). Individualism in a collectivist culture: A case of coexistence of the opposites. In U. Kim, H.C. Triandis, C. Kagitcibasi, S.C. Choi, and G. Yoon (Eds), *Individualism and Collectivism: Theory, Method and Application* (pp. 123–36). Thousand Oaks, CA: Sage.

Sinha, J. (1961). *Indian Psychology,* Vol. 3. Calcutta: Jadunath Sinha Foundation.

Sinha, J. (1958). *Indian Psychology,* Vol. 1 and 2. Calcutta: Jadunath Sinha Foundation.

Sinha, J.B.P. (2014). *Psycho-Social Analysis of the Indian Mindset.* New Delhi: Springer.

Sinha, J.B.P. (2002). Towards indigenization of psychology in India. In G. Misra and A.K. Mohanty (Eds), *Perspectives on Indigenous Psychology* (pp. 440–57). New Delhi: Concept.

Sinha, J.B.P. (2000a). Indigenization of psychology in India. *Psychological Studies*, 45, 3–13.

Sinha, J.B.P. (2000b). *Patterns of Work Culture: Cases and Strategies for Culture Building*. New Delhi: Sage.

Sinha, J.B.P. (1993). The front and the bulk of Indian psychology. *Psychology and Developing Societies*, 5, 135–50.

Sinha, J.B.P. (1990). *Work Culture in the Indian Context*. New Delhi: Sage.

Sinha, J.B.P. (1984). Towards partnership for relevant research in the third world. *International Journal of Psychology*, 19, 169–77.

Sinha, J.B.P. (1980). *Nurturant Task Leader.* New Delhi: Concept.

Sinha, J.B.P. (1973). Methodology of problem-oriented research in India. *Journal of Social and Economic Studies*, 1, 93–110.

Sinha, J.B.P. (1970). Construct of dependence proneness. *Journal of Social Psychology*, 76 (1), 129–31.

Snyder, C.R. and Lopez, S. (2002). *Handbook of Positive Psychology*. New York: Academic Press.

Sri Aurobindo. (1939/2006). *The Life Divine*. Puducherry: Sri Aurobindo Ashram.

Srivastava, A.K. and Misra, G. (2003). Going beyond the model of economic man: An indigenous perspective on happiness. *Journal of Indian Psychology*, 21, 12–29.

Stanley, L. (Ed.). (1990). *Feminist Praxis: Research, Theory and Epistemology in Feminist Sociology*. London: Routledge.

Swami Rama, Ballentine, R. and Ajaya, S. (1976). *Yoga and Psychotherapy*. Honesdale, PA: Himalayan Institute.

Tart, C. (2009). *The End of Materialism*. Oakland, CA: Neotic Books.

Tart, C. (1975). *Transpersonal Psychologies*. San Francisco: Harper & Row.

Tayal, O.P. (1970). Visual processing: General principles for an interpretation of geometrical illusions. *Journal of General Psychology*, 86, 93–115.

Thapar, R. (2002). *The Penguin History of Early India*. New Delhi: Penguin.

Triandis, H.C. (1984). Toward a psychological theory of economic growth. *International Journal of Psychology*, 19, 79–96.

Triandis, H.C. (1980). Introduction. In H.C. Triandis and W.W. Lambert (Eds), *Handbook of Cross-Cultural Psychology: Perspective,* Vol. 1 (pp. 15–30). Boston: Allyn & Bacon.

Tripathi, R.C. (1989, September). *Psychology as a Policy Science*. Paper presented at the Seminar on Psychology as a Policy Science. University of Allhabad, Allahabad.

Tripathi, R.C. (1988). Aligning development to values in India. In D. Sinha and H.S.R. Kao (Eds), *Social Values and Development: Asian Perspectives* (pp. 315–33). New Delhi: Sage.

UGC. (1999). *Curriculum in Psychology*. New Delhi: University Grants Commission.

UGC. (1985). *UGC Annual Report, 1983–84*. New Delhi: University Grants Commission.

UGC. (1982). *Status of Psychology in Indian Universities*. New Delhi: University Grants Commission.

UGC. (1968). *Psychology in Indian Universities*. New Delhi: University Grants Commission.

Vahali, H.O. (2009). *Lives in Exile: Exploring the Inner World of Tibetan Refugees*. New Delhi: Routledge.

Vaidyanathan, T.J. and Kripal, J.J. (1999). *Vishnu on the Desk of Freud*. New Delhi: Oxford University Press.

Vanden Bos, G.R. (Ed.). (1996). Outcome assessment of psychotherapy. *American Psychologist*, 51(10).

Varma, M. (1976). *Moral Development in Children*. Allahabad: Chug Publications.

Varma, P.K. (2004). *Being Indian*. New Delhi: Penguin.

Varma, S. (2004). Psychology in India: Past trends and future possibilities. In K. Joshi and M. Cornelissen (Eds), *Consciousness, Indian Psychology and Yoga*, Vol. 11, Part 3, (pp. 224–36). New Delhi: Centre for Studies in Civilizations.

Varma, S. (2002). Demystifying scientism in mainstream psychology. In G. Misra and A. Mohanty (Eds), *Perspectives on Indigenous Psychology* (pp. 37–66). New Delhi: Concept.

Verghese, A. (1973). A social and psychiatric study of a representative group of families in Vellore town. *Indian Journal of Medical Research*, 61, 609–20.

Vindhya, U. (Ed.). (2003). *Psychology in India: Intersecting Crossroads*. New Delhi: Concept Publications.

Vishwanathan, S. (1998). A celebrations of difference: Science and democracy in India. *Science*, 280, 42–43.

Vishwanathan, S. (1995). *A Carnival for Science*. New Delhi: Oxford University Press.

Wertz, F.J. (1998). The role of the humanistic movement in the history of psychology. *Journal of Humanistic Psychology*, 38(1), 42–70.

Wig, N.N. and Akhtar, S. (1974). Twenty-five years of psychiatric research in India. *Indian Journal of Psychiatry*, 16, 48–64.

Willig, C. and Staintaton-Rogers, W. (2008). *Sage Handbook of Qualitative Research in Psychology*. London: Sage.

Worchel, S. and Cooper, J. (1989). *Understanding Social Psychology*. Homewood, IL: The Dorsey Press.

Index